The Labor Spy Racket

A Da Capo Press Reprint Series

CIVIL LIBERTIES IN AMERICAN HISTORY

GENERAL EDITOR: LEONARD W. LEVY

Claremont Graduate School

The
Labor Spy Racket

BY LEO HUBERMAN

DA CAPO PRESS · NEW YORK · 1971

A Da Capo Press Reprint Edition

This Da Capo Press edition of
The Labor Spy Racket
is an unabridged republication of the
first edition published in New York in 1937.

Library of Congress Catalog Card Number 77-139201
SBN 306-70080-8

Published by Da Capo Press
A Division of Plenum Publishing Corporation
227 West 17th Street, New York, N.Y. 10011

Manufactured in the United States of America

The Labor Spy Racket

by the same author

"WE, THE PEOPLE"

MAN'S WORLDLY GOODS

The
Labor Spy Racket

BY LEO HUBERMAN

MODERN AGE BOOKS, INC., NEW YORK

Composed and printed in the United States of America by Union Labor
AT THE RUMFORD PRESS, CONCORD, NEW HAMPSHIRE

Typography by Robert Josephy

First printing September 1937
Second printing September 1937

To Sybil, Aileen, and Roger,
staunch trade unionists

CONTENTS

ILLUSTRATIONS

PREFACE

MOST of the material in this book is based on the evidence introduced in the hearings before the Subcommittee of the Committee on
Education and Labor of the United States Senate, popularly
known as the La Follette Civil Liberties Committee. The hearings
were reported in the press, but for obvious reasons the press accounts could not be full enough. The complete text has been printed
by the Government Printing Office — 2,500,000 words of stenographic records to date, published in eight volumes with perhaps
twice that number still to come. An obvious need, lest this vitally
important material be buried on committee shelves, was a short
book that would fall between the too-short newspaper account and
the too-long stenographic record.

I have tried to write such a book. My task, as I saw it, was to
become thoroughly familiar with the complete text and select
therefrom, and then organize, those highlights that tell the story.
It is a shocking story. It is a story which should shame our industrialists and arouse our workers. It is a story which should cause all
fair-minded Americans to rise up in their wrath and demand that
immediate steps be taken to prevent what has happened here from
ever happening again.

Only that part of the committee's work which pertains to Labor
Spies is dealt with in these pages. The related topics of strike-
breaking and industry's traffic in tear gas and munitions receive
little attention, primarily because they have been so fully treated in
I Break Strikes by Edward Levinson, and because it was important
to keep the book as short and simple as possible.

I am deeply indebted to the following for their advice and help:
Max Lerner, David J. Saposs, Edwin S. Smith, and my wife.

LEO HUBERMAN

New York, June 1937

I. $80,000,000 a Year for Spies

FOR TEN YEARS Richard Frankensteen had been a trimmer in the Dodge plant of the Chrysler Corporation in Detroit. He had followed in the footsteps of his father who had worked for the Dodge Corporation for many years before and had been a leader in the plant band. Frankensteen was popular with the other employees in the trim division and in 1934 they elected him as their representative in the Chrysler Corporation Representation Plan. At a meeting of the representatives of the other divisions, Frankensteen was elected as chairman of the whole section. It was not long before he and the other representatives learned that their Works Council had definite limitations: collective bargaining under this company union plan meant that the men could ask for and get better lighting, a larger milk bottle, improved ventilation, and similar concessions. But beyond these they could not go. When it came to collective bargaining for higher wages, shorter hours, seniority rights, etc., the employee representation plan failed them.

The representatives decided to get together and call meetings of their constituents to see what could be done. The outcome of these meetings of the Chrysler workers was the formation of a union of their own, the Automotive Industrial Workers Association. Fourteen locals of the A.I.W.A. were organized in the Dodge plant and Richard Frankensteen was elected president. At the same time, Frankensteen, along with the other representatives, continued his services in the Chrysler employee representation plan. The workers had both a company union and their own union.

Frankensteen was a hardworking president. He attended the meetings of the fourteen locals and made speeches to the members. One night in 1934, after a speech to the members of the paint local,

3

Frankensteen was driven home in the car of the vice president of the local, John Andrews. This was the beginning of a warm friendship. Andrews became Frankensteen's most trusted companion. Richard wanted more than anything else to create a strong union composed of militant wideawake members, and he naturally took to John who was fearless, uncompromising, and able. John was a strong union man; he harangued the men for hours and gave them courage to go out on strike when conditions grew too bad; he was the leader on the picket line; he drove Richard around in his car to union meetings at any and all hours. Richard felt that he could depend on John to devote every moment of his spare time to the formation of that powerful body of militant unionized workers which was Richard's sole ambition.

Both men were married and had two children. The families, living less than ten blocks apart, became very friendly. John's wife, Dee, and her two children, were frequent visitors at the Frankensteen home. While Carol-Lee and Marilyn Frankensteen played with Ronnie and Dale Andrews, Richard's wife, Mickey, and Dee Andrews would go on shopping trips together. When Dee was sick Mickey brought over some custard she had made and took care of Ronnie and Dale. On another occasion John and Dee drove Mickey and the babies to and from her parents' home in Dayton, where all of them stayed together in the old folks' house and had a grand two day visit. Five nights a week and all day Sunday the two men rode around together busy with their union work, but every Saturday night was set aside regularly for Fun — a joint good time when the two wives with their husbands met for dinner and the movies. In the summer of 1935 when the plant was shut down for a few weeks, the two families went to Lake Orion for a vacation. They took a house together and shared expenses. The Andrews and the Frankensteens were firm fast friends for the two years following that night in 1934 when John Andrews first shook hands with Richard Frankensteen after his speech at the meeting of the paint local.

Yet every day for the whole period of their friendship, John Andrews wrote a detailed report of the activities of his pal, Dick Frankensteen. John Andrews was a spy. He sent his reports to the office of the Corporations Auxiliary Co., a private detective agency hired by the Chrysler Corporation. For spying on his friend Frankensteen and his other fellow workers, John Andrews was paid $40 a month by the Corporations Auxiliary. For the services of its spy, L-392 (the code number of John Andrews), Corporations Auxiliary billed the Chrysler Corporation at the rate of $9.00 per day. And for the services of all its undercover operatives in 1935, Corporations Auxiliary was paid by the Chrysler Corporation the sum of $72,611.89.

From that last figure — the payment to one detective agency by one corporation in one year — it becomes obvious that the story of John Andrews and Richard Frankensteen is more than the story of a friend betrayed. It is the story of a big business. John Andrews was one operative of one agency. There are hundreds of agencies employing thousands of operatives in the United States. There are agency chains with branch offices in many large industrial centers. Their undercover operatives are at work in every part of the country in every industry. It is impossible to obtain exact figures for either the number of agencies or their operatives. They operate in secret and never divulge more information than they have to about their business. In the hearings before the Subcommittee of the Committee on Education and Labor of the United States Senate — the La Follette Civil Liberties Committee — they were very unwilling witnesses. They lied frequently and suffered from partial and complete loss of memory throughout. However, Mr. Heber Blankenhorn, industrial economist on the National Labor Relations Board, was able to furnish the committee with a list he had compiled after twenty years of study of industrial espionage. Mr. Blankenhorn is the foremost authority on the subject in the United States. Here is his list from the record:

    As of April 1936
    Total agencies.................... 230 [Turn to Appendix
                                        A for complete list].

Systems:

Cities

William J. Burns, International Detective Agency, Inc. 43
Pinkerton's National Detective Agency 35
Railway Audit and Inspection Co., with affiliates
(known to be incomplete) 18
Corporations Auxiliary Co. (known to be incomplete) 8
Sherman Service, Inc. 9

How many operatives these 230 agencies employ is still a mystery. Estimates vary from 40,000 for all of them to 135,000 for just the Burns, Pinkerton, and Thiel agencies alone. The minimum figure is based on the fact that there are some 41,000 union locals in the United States and it is estimated that *there is a spy in every local.* One labor leader with many years of experience states that he never "knew of a gathering large enough to be called a meeting and small enough to exclude the spy."

What is the cost to industry of this countrywide spy service? How much of the money that you pay for the milk you drink, the car you drive, the clothing you wear, the furniture you use, the food you eat, went to paying the miserable wages of the stool-pigeons and the fabulous salaries of the agency heads? We don't know exactly, but even the lowest estimate will astound you. Mr. Blankenhorn, figuring an average of $175 a month paid to the agency per spy, and 40,000 spies, computes the minimum cost at over $80,-000,000 per year! That this is probably too low an estimate was indicated in the hearings before the committee when General Motors officials testified that their plants had paid to Pinkertons alone, $419,850.10, for the period from January 1934 through July 1936; and that they paid to all the agencies they hired in that period a total of $994,855.68! Small wonder that so many detective agencies have given up shadowing criminals and have turned their attention to selling what they euphemistically call their "industrial service." They have found that there is more money in industry than in crime.

Who are the clients of these detective agencies? Here is a partial list of the customers:

Employers' associations............................ 36
Corporations of nationwide scope................... 14
Railroads... 27
Tractions, utilities, bus companies.................... 29
Metallurgy and machinery.......................... 52
Mining.. 32
Auto industry..................................... 28
Clothing, silk, and textile mills..................... 29
Steamship lines................................... 20
Radio and refrigerators............................ 9
Food... 28
Shoe and leather.................................. 11
Building, supplies, etc............................. 7
Milling... 8
Department and clothing stores..................... 7
Publishers and printing............................ 5
Real estate....................................... 6
Trucking, delivery, warehousing.................... 17
Lumber, woodworking.............................. 3
Hotels and theaters................................ 9
Banking, trust and security........................ 5
Miscellaneous.................................... 47
                                                   ───
    Total.. 429

A breakdown of that list will reveal some names of companies which are well known to you. For example, among the 499 clients in 19 states of the Corporations Auxiliary Co. in the period 1934–1936 were the following:

Aluminum Co. of America	Crane Co.
American Book Co.	Diamond Match Co.
Chrysler Corp. (23 plants)	Dixie Greyhound Lines

Firestone Tire and Rubber Co.
General Motors Corporation
and subsidiaries (13 plants)
International Shoe Co.
Kellogg Co.
Kelvinator Corp.

Midland Steel Products Co.
New York Edison Co.
Postum Co.
Quaker Oats Co.
Radio Corp. of America
Standard Oil Co.

Statler Hotels, Inc.

The Pinkerton Agency, in the years 1933–1936, "serviced" these familiar firms, among many others:

Abbott's Dairies
Bethlehem Steel Co.
Campbell Soup Co.
Continental Can Co.
Curtis Publishing Co.
Endicott-Johnson Corp.
Libbey-Owens Ford Glass Co.

Montgomery Ward & Co.
National Cash Register Co.
Ohrbach's Affiliated Stores
Pennsylvania R. R. Co.
Shell Petroleum Corp.
Sinclair Refining Co.
United Shoe Machinery Corp.

And among the mutilated records of the Railway Audit and Inspection Co., the following names appeared:

Borden Milk Co.
Carnegie-Illinois Steel Corporation ⎰ subsidiaries of
H. C. Frick Coal and Coke Co.   ⎱ United States Steel
Consolidated Gas Co. of New York
Frigidaire Corp.
Jewish Hospital, Brooklyn, N. Y.
Pennsylvania Greyhound Bus Co.
Western Union
Westinghouse Electric & Manufacturing Co.

These are only a few of the clients of three of the agencies. A complete list covering all the agencies would contain hundreds of other names. Big firms and small firms, old firms and new firms, famous firms headed by famous people and unknown firms headed by unknown people — all are subscribers to the "industrial service" of these private detective agencies.

II. Smash the Union!

NOW $80,000,000 a year is a lot of money.

When the detective agencies sell their industrial service, what are they selling? What do their customers get in return for the $80,000,-000 a year?

You would think that the quickest and easiest way of having that question answered would be to ask the people who buy the service and the people who sell it. Senator La Follette and Senator Thomas tried that. But they found that this was a peculiar business. The people who knew most about it wouldn't talk. They were very secretive. They destroyed many of their records. Often they didn't hear the question — or when they did hear it, they didn't understand it. They beat around the bush. They were shifty unwilling witnesses. They lied frequently. Nevertheless, there were times when the evidence was so overwhelming, that they had to come clean. Backed into a corner from which there was no escape they had to confess to the truth. And bit by bit, the story did come out. Salvaged records, indiscreet letters, confessions by spies, confessions by operatives, admissions by plant managers — all were piled up until the broad outlines of the business and many of the details, were clear. We know now what the private detective agencies sold.

They sold a unique service — Union-Prevention and Union-Smashing. Industrialists who bought the service wanted to know about their workers' attempts to organize. They paid $80,000,000 a year to keep their plants from becoming unionized, or if they were unionized, to break up the union. There is no longer any doubt about it. The record is clear.

Here, for example, is part of a letter from the Foster Service to a prospective client:

Your letter of July 28 is received. With reference to your inquiry about my experience and what I am prepared to do in case of disturbance, etc.

First, I will say that if we are employed before any union or organization is formed by the employees, there will be no strike and no disturbance. This does not say there will be no unions formed, but it does say that we will control the activities of the union and direct its policies, provided we are allowed a free hand by our clients.

Second. If a union is already formed and no strike is on or expected to be declared within 30 or 60 days, although we are not in the same position as we would be in the above case, we could — and I believe with success — carry on an intrigue which would result in factions, disagreements, resignations of officers, and general decrease in the membership.

That's plain and to the point. Another letter, from the Marshall Detective Service Company to the Red Star Milling Company of Wichita, Kansas, was equally precise. It is especially interesting because in it the agency found it necessary to explain something that might have puzzled the client: the Red Star Company was paying for Union-Smashing, yet the reports it received from the agency showed that the operative was about to become an officer in the union! It looked like the doublecross, but the agency assures the client that everything is O.K.:

You have doubtless learned from the reports that our No. 20 is likely to be elected Recording Secretary of the Local in Wichita, and for fear that you may not understand this in the right light, we wish to advise you that all of our Operatives are instructed to accept the office of Recording Secretary if possible; as the Recording Secretary has nothing to do with agitation, simply keeping the records which are valuable to us, and from which we obtain all our information. You will understand that if No. 20 is elected to this office he will be in a position to give the name and record of every man who belongs to the union, and as to whether or not he pays his dues, and attends the meetings regular, and all the inside information that we desire.

The only office in the Union that we bar our men from accepting is that of Business Agent. The Office of Business Agent is the only office in the union, which can harm the mills, as it is the duty of the Business Agent to induce the men to join the Union, and as it is not our policy to induce men to join the Union, but to endeavor to keep them from joining, our Operatives are naturally barred from accepting the office of Business Agent . . .

We trust that you will fully understand this matter and if No. 20 is elected, he will be instructed to take any orders from you which you may think will benefit the mill and endeavor to carry them out in the Union, and as an Officer in the Local his views will carry more weight with your men than they would otherwise.

That was written in 1919. The Foster Service letter was written in 1920. Has the service changed much since then? Not very much according to Mr. James H. Smith, president of the Corporations Auxiliary Co. He ought to know because he has been in the business about 40 years. Senator La Follette asked Mr. Smith, when he was on the witness stand, whether there had been many changes since he originally came into the business. Here is his answer, "Well, I think it has changed slightly, but not very much. We have gone into the efficiency end of it more definitely and particularly as the years have gone by."

But though the business hasn't changed much the method of describing it has. The agency heads no longer commit themselves as openly as they once did. They rarely make the mistake of allowing themselves such complete frankness as in the past. In 1910 the Corporations Auxiliary Co. could inform a client that "wherever our system has been in operation for a reasonable length of time, considering the purpose to be accomplished, the result has been that union membership has not increased, if our clients wished otherwise. In many cases local union charters have been returned without publicity and a number of local unions have been disbanded. We help eliminate the agitator and organizer quietly and with little or no friction."

But in 1937 Mr. Smith wasn't writing or talking so plainly. He was much more guarded. When he was asked to describe his agency's work at the La Follette hearings, he talked glibly about selling the services of his "industrial engineers" — but he had to admit that not one of his men was an engineer. Here is Mr. Smith on the witness stand:

SENATOR LA FOLLETTE. What type of business are these companies engaged in, Mr. Smith?

MR. SMITH. They are engaged in the business of assisting manufacturers in increasing and improving their products both in quantity and quality and reducing their operating costs. That is their primary business.

SENATOR LA FOLLETTE. And how is that accomplished?

MR. SMITH. Well, it is accomplished on a very simple process. We feel that in order to get efficiency and to get a good product the first thing you have to have is harmony, if you can possibly get it, because without harmony you get no efficiency or anything else, and therefore we sometimes say we assist in harmonizing conditions in a plant.

The change from 1910 is apparent. Then you knew without any question what service Corporations Auxiliary performed. In 1937, Mr. Smith uses honeyed words, "we assist in harmonizing conditions in a plant." That sounds nice but what does it mean? The testimony of Mr. Herman Weckler, vice president and general manager of the De Soto Motor Corporation, a Chrysler subsidiary, gives us a clue. Remember that the Chrysler Corporation was Corporation Auxiliary's biggest customer:

SENATOR LA FOLLETTE. Did you receive reports and did these reports, while you were receiving them, give information on meetings of union locals in which employees of the Chrysler plants were members?

MR. WECKLER. Yes, sir.

.   .   .

SENATOR LA FOLLETTE. Did you receive reports on meetings of the district council of the United Automobile Workers?

MR. WECKLER. I think I have seen one or two of those, yes.

SENATOR LA FOLLETTE. And did they report on the meetings of the Society of Designing Engineers?

MR. WECKLER. I saw reports from the Society.

.   .   .

SENATOR LA FOLLETTE. Through these reports, then, it is a fair statement to say that you are kept fully informed as to the strategy and plans of these locals and this district organization, is it not?

MR. WECKLER. Yes, sir.

If you want convincing proof of how very well informed Mr. Weckler was of the union activities of the auto workers, just turn to Appendix B, and read the kind of detailed spy report he was receiving from Corporations Auxiliary. From Mr. Weckler's testimony and from this sample spy report, we gather that Corporations Auxiliary's 1937 model of "harmonizing conditions," was in no sense different from its 1910 model of union-smashing.

Mr. Smith, president of Corporations Auxiliary, was an unwilling, evasive witness. His general manager, Mr. Dan Ross, was more willing but equally slippery. Mr. Ross picked up Smith's "harmonizing conditions," and added to it "promoting efficiency" as his descriptive term for the spying activities of his stool-pigeons. Like Smith, Ross was careful to talk all around the subject but very little directly on it. But both Smith and Ross were long-winded as compared to the tight-lipped Pinkertons. The heads of this agency doing a million dollar a year business could remember almost nothing at all, and what they did remember always had precious little to do with reporting on the union activities of their clients' workers.

One afternoon when six of the agency heads were sitting on the stand tossing the questions around to one another in their usual fashion, a newspaper man sent up a note to Mr. Robert Wohlforth, the able secretary of the committee: The note read,

> Six little Pinks sitting in a row,
> Six little Pinks and none of them know.

That's bad poetry but it's good reporting. Judge for yourself:

SENATOR LA FOLLETTE. Mr. Pinkerton, will you take a look at that exhibit, please [Pinkerton journal sheet], and tell me what kind of information you would say the agency would try to get for the United States Rubber Reclaiming Company?

MR. PINKERTON. Information dealing with sabotage, theft of material, and other irregularities.

SENATOR LA FOLLETTE. What would you include under "sabotage"?

MR. PINKERTON. Damage to company property.

SENATOR LA FOLLETTE. Anything else?

MR. PINKERTON. No, not if you take that in a general term.

SENATOR LA FOLLETTE. It goes on to say "also thefts of material." That is pretty obvious. But what about "and other irregularities"? What would you say that includes?

MR. PINKERTON. That could include a great many things.

SENATOR LA FOLLETTE. What would it usually include?

MR. PINKERTON. Probably discrimination, favoritism by the minor officials in the plant, and violation of rules and regulations.

[Senator La Follette then reads a report of a Pinkerton spy, dated May 16, 1936, *describing a union meeting* * attended by some workers of the United States Rubber Reclaiming Company, Buffalo, N. Y.]

SENATOR LA FOLLETTE. Would you say that this report had to do with investigation of sabotage of the company's property, theft or other irregularities?

---

* Italics here and throughout the book are the author's.

MR. PINKERTON. No, sir.

SENATOR LA FOLLETTE. What would you say, Mr. Rossetter, about that?

MR. ROSSETTER [vice president and general manager]. I would say that it did not touch those points, but my impression is that that was a "Red" organization. I am not familiar with the names of the different units comprising the Communist Party or its supporters, but that report would cover —

SENATOR LA FOLLETTE (interrupting). Would you say it had anything to do with the investigation of sabotage of the company's property, theft of materials, or other irregularities?

MR. ROSSETTER. It might lead to sabotage if those people were the kind that I think they may be — Communists.

SENATOR LA FOLLETTE. Now, Mr. Rossetter, isn't it true that the description, in the Pinkerton journal, of sabotage, theft and irregularity, often actually covers up investigations to be made of union activities?

. . .

MR. ROSSETTER. Well, if you can take that as a sample, I will have to say "yes" to it . . .

SENATOR LA FOLLETTE. As a matter of fact, did not the agency undertake to report on the activities of unions within this plant and organizational efforts of the client's employees?

MR. ROSSETTER. I have no personal knowledge of that, Senator. I could not say one way or the other.

SENATOR LA FOLLETTE. Do you know about it, Mr. Dudley?

MR. DUDLEY [assistant general manager]. The only ones who would know about that, I presume, would be the division manager and the superintendent.

SENATOR LA FOLLETTE. Do you think the client would know what he hired you for, Mr. Pinkerton?

MR. PINKERTON. I should think he would; yes, sir.

SENATOR LA FOLLETTE. I now offer an exhibit. It is a letter from L. J. Plumb, of the United States Rubber Reclaiming Co. to Charles F. Smith, dated August 5, 1935, re Pinkerton

Agency. It is on the stationery of an interoffice memorandum and is as follows:

"I have yours of the 2nd in reference to this subject. You do not, however, tell me whether they have given you any information of value or importance.

"What have their reports amounted to?

Very truly yours,

U. S. RUBBER RECLAIMING CO., INC.

L. J. Plumb, *President.*"

On the back of this exhibit . . . is the reply:

8/6/35

"*Dear Mr. Plumb:* The information contained in the Pinkerton reports has not resulted in any direct saving or profit. They cover the activities of both unions and report any meetings or other activities involving our employees or the rubber workers in this district. As stated in my letter of August 2nd I consider this about the best arrangement that we could make for being informed of such activities.

C. F. SMITH"

SENATOR LA FOLLETTE. It would indicate that your client, Mr. Pinkerton, was actually interested in organizational activities, would it not?

MR. PINKERTON. Yes, sir; it would.

SENATOR LA FOLLETTE. And it is obvious that your Buffalo office agreed to furnish the names of the employees of the client who were active in union activities, is it not?

. . .

MR. PINKERTON. This does not say that any names of employees are being furnished.

SENATOR LA FOLLETTE. Well, did they furnish that information?

MR. PINKERTON. I do not know.

SENATOR LA FOLLETTE. Well, let us read this next exhibit:

"Informant reports:

Tuesday, March 19, 1935.

"At headquarters of the Rubber Workers' Industrial Union and the Trades Union Unity League, Charles Doyle, J. J. Kissell, Angello Bustini, and several other members were heard to say a meeting of the employees of the U. S. Rubber Reclaiming Co. was held secretly at Liberty Hall, Jefferson and Bristol Sts., last evening, which was well attended and three members enrolled.

"It was learned that B. Brewer, Earl Ericks, John Jackson, Willard Dunsmore and Herbert Zmanski, all employees of the U. S. Rubber Reclaiming Co., have agreed to serve on the organization committee."

Now the fact that the Pinkertons thus tried in every way to conceal the true character of their "industrial service" is not important. What is important is for us to understand what the nature of that work was. There is no doubt that some of the operatives were indeed reporting on "sabotage, theft, and other irregularities." There is also no doubt that many of the operatives were reporting on the union activities of the workers. The record shouts the story — spy agencies are hired primarily for the purpose of keeping the employer informed of any and all attempts on the part of the workers in a plant to better their conditions through organization; and to use any means, fair or foul, to destroy that organization.

For further proof let us turn to the testimony of the men who did the job, the spies themselves. Mr. William H. Martin was a Pinkerton operative for seven years, from 1928 to 1935. Here is part of his sworn testimony:

SENATOR THOMAS. What was your next industrial job, Mr. Martin?

MR. MARTIN. That was with the Harmony Bus Line, Pittsburgh, Pa.

SENATOR THOMAS. Detailed for what purpose?

MR. MARTIN. Detailed by Mr. Reed, superintendent at

Pittsburgh, to ride a certain man named McDonald, who was a bus driver for this company, ride him out of town for about a 40 minute ride to Allison Park. I was to get acquainted with him, start talking to him, get some information as to what they were doing, whether they were organizing, who the men were that were going to join the union, anything I could get pertaining to their unionization.

SENATOR THOMAS. Did you know who Mr. McDonald was?

MR. MARTIN. I had heard he was the chairman of the organizing committee for this company.

SENATOR THOMAS. You definitely realized you were on a labor spying job?

MR. MARTIN. Yes, sir.

SENATOR THOMAS. Did Reed tell you why he wanted the information?

MR. MARTIN. Mr. Reed said they were having some trouble over there, the men were going to organize and the company was not in a position to pay union drivers.

. . .

SENATOR THOMAS. The trouble was that the men were going to organize?

MR. MARTIN. Yes, sir.

SENATOR THOMAS. That was conceded as a trouble?

MR. MARTIN. Yes, sir; and they wanted some information to do away with that.

SENATOR THOMAS. What kind of information were you instructed to obtain, definitely?

MR. MARTIN. To obtain information as to who the men were that were going to join the union . . .

The General Motors Corporation and its subsidiaries were clients of the Pinkerton Agency. One of the workers in the Chevrolet plant in Atlanta, Georgia, was Mr. Lyle Letteer, the son of the assistant superintendent of the Atlanta office of the Pinkerton agency. In April 1934 he was employed as a Pinkerton spy while continuing his work in the plant. Mr. Letteer was instructed to join the union and report on its financial condition, its paid-up members, and the names of the Chevrolet employees who were union members. He was told to get himself elected as an officer in the union and make a detailed report on its secret meetings. In the summer of 1935 he was able to perform a major stroke as a spy. The other officers of the union were attending a convention in Detroit and Mr. Letteer was left in charge of the office. What a break! That he made the most of his opportunity is plain from his sworn testimony:

SENATOR LA FOLLETTE. Did you take advantage of that situation of being left as the sole person in charge and responsible for these records, to make use of them for Pinkerton?

MR. LETTEER. I took advantage to this extent, that after asking Littlejohn [Pinkerton superintendent] what he wanted to know and receiving his answer, I went to the labor office and as I was going to close up for the night I would take all the records, including the ledger and everything, whatever he called for for that day, take it to the office, and we would make copies that night.

SENATOR LA FOLLETTE. You mean to the Pinkerton office?

MR. LETTEER. Yes, sir.

SENATOR LA FOLLETTE. Then you returned the records to the office the next morning?

MR. LETTEER. Returned the records to the office next morning.

SENATOR LA FOLLETTE. State, if you know, what use the Pinkerton Agency made of all this information that you were able to get as a result of your position of trust in this union?

MR. LETTEER. The exact use of it I could not say but it seemed to be pretty hot as far as Littlejohn would say.

The scene now shifts to Michigan. Pinkerton still on the job for General Motors. Mr. Lawrence Barker of Detroit is taken on as a Pinkerton spy (after a few months, he confessed to the union officials and two letters are in the record attesting their faith in him) and is planted in the Fisher Body factory in Lansing. His

superior officer is Mr. R. S. Mason, assistant superintendent of the
Detroit office of the Pinkerton Agency. We learn from Mr. Mason's
talks with Mr. Barker that pinching the records from a union office
is only one way of keeping tab on union activities — there are other
Pinkerton methods, equally efficient. Here is Mr. Barker on the
witness stand:

SENATOR LA FOLLETTE. In these discussions that you had
with Mr. Mason, did you get the impression or did you know
that he knew a good deal about the activities of the international union, as well as the various locals?

MR. BARKER. He did seem to know quite a bit about the
activities of the international.

. . .

SENATOR LA FOLLETTE. Did he ever tell you how he happened
to know so much about the union and its activities?

MR. BARKER. Yes, sir, he said that they had a dummy office
in the Hoffman Building [United Automobile Workers Association headquarters in Detroit], that the telephone there was
tapped, and also President Martin's telephone was tapped at
his home. That they knew everything about him and every
move they would make.

. . .

SENATOR LA FOLLETTE. Mr. Barker, as the result of your experience as an undercover operator, informant and spy, what is
your impression about the effectiveness or lack of effectiveness
of this labor espionage work in breaking up or preventing
unions, genuine labor unions, from organizing?

MR. BARKER. It is very effective, especially in the local to
which I belonged . . . One time at Lansing-Fisher they were
almost 100 per cent organized. And finally it went down to
where, as I said, there were only five officers left.

SENATOR LA FOLLETTE. You attribute that to undercover
operatives?

MR. BARKER. Yes; I do.

Mr. Barker testifies, from experience, that labor espionage has been very effective in breaking up unions. He gives, as an example, the smashing of the Lansing-Fisher local. Affidavits of similar happenings in other unions are strewn throughout the pages of the record. From the testimony of Robert Travis, organizer for the United Automobile Workers, the committee learned of a Federal Labor Union in Flint, *which had shrunk from a membership of 26,000 in 1935, to 122 in 1936* — wrecked by union officials who were spies.

The spy who has become an official in the union is, of course, in a key position to wreak havoc with the organization. The more capable he is, the more dangerous he is. Some spies have been able to reach the top — and all the way up they have been doing their deadly work. William Green, president of the A. F. of L., testified that a spy named L. E. Woodward had become president of the Savannah Trades and Labor Council, vice president of the Georgia Federation of Labor for 4 years, and had even been nominated for president at the state convention of the A. F. of L.! His reports, meanwhile, went regularly through the Pinkerton Agency to the Savannah Electric and Power Company, and probably, to every other company in Georgia that subscribed to the Pinkerton service.

The extent to which labor unions are infected with the plague of spies is so widespread as almost to exceed belief. If some of the authentic tales had been invented they could not have sounded more fantastic. The following story, however, has been proven true: in November 1935, the American Federation of Labor, in an effort to collect all the information it could about spies, sent a questionnaire to its locals throughout the country. Here are the questions asked and the answers received from Local 18920, in Hartford, Conn.:

American Federation of Labor Questionnaire November 30, 1935.

1. What spy and strikebreaking agencies operate in your territory or industry? — A. Pinkerton's National Detective

Agency, R. W. Bridgman Detective Bureau, Hartford Private Detective Bureau (listed from phone directory).

2. Which are most active since the passage of the Wagner Act? — A. No knowledge.

3. Give names of agencies, addresses and, if possible, names of chief officers. — A. See no. 1.

4. How many operatives or spies do agencies have? — A. No knowledge.

5. What exposures of spies among your membership have been made by your union? Or in the courts? — A. None in our local. One employee of Fuller Brush Company exposed as spy.

6. If possible, give full account of facts. — A. All facts in possession of President W. Kuehnel, Hartford Central Labor Union.

7. What activities are spy agencies carrying on? — A. No knowledge.

8. Have they organized 'citizens' committees'? — A. Not to my knowledge.

9. What industrial concerns are known to have employed spy agencies? — A. Fuller Brush Company.

10. What precise information have you as to large industrial concerns' own spy system? — A. None.

11. Which agencies at present supply strikebreakers? How many have they recruited (give instances)? — A. None, to best of my knowledge.

Re resolution no. 168.

Name of union: Typewriter Workers Local No. 18920.

Secretary: F. A. Roszel.

Address: 2 Wolcott Avenue, Wilson, Conn.

Notice that the secretary of this Hartford local is not very helpful — more than half the questions are answered "no knowledge." This reply was received at A. F. of L. headquarters on December 11, 1935. One week later the picture of Mr. F. A. Roszel, the secretary of the local, was published. He was a spy. When he came to

Hartford in 1934, the paid membership of the local of which he later became secretary was 2500. In less than one year, the paid membership had dropped to 75, with a regular attendance of not more than 8 or 10 members! Mr. Roszel had done a swell job for the International Auxiliary (a subsidiary of Corporations Auxiliary).

There is bitter irony in this story of an A. F. of L. questionnaire on spies being answered by a union secretary who was himself a spy. Equally ironical — and significant — was the evidence given by Mr. Matthew Smith, general secretary of the Mechanics Educational Society of America, a union of tool and die makers, to President Roosevelt's joint N.R.A. and Labor Department inquiry into employment stabilization. *The New York Times* of December 17, 1934, reported Mr. Smith as testifying that "several weeks ago he had inadvertently lost a copy of the minutes of his union meeting and he had received an even more detailed statement of what had transpired at the meeting from a detective agency which had 'covered' the meeting through its own operative"!

Was it merely a coincidence that of the 30 operatives employed out of the Cleveland office of Corporations Auxiliary in November 1935, "23 were members of unions, 2 were not members of unions at the plant, and the remaining 5 were non-union men employed at plants where no union had been organized"?

The Pinkertons, according to a schedule they themselves submitted to the committee, did not have as high a percentage of their operatives in unions, but what their operatives lacked in union affiliations, they made up in influence as high ranking union officials.

The summary of this schedule, prepared by Pinkerton's National Detective Agency, Inc. [March 16, 1937] is as follows:

Total number of secret sources carried under arbitrary or secret designations — 303.

Of this number,

132 are members of trade unions,

43 are members of company unions or employee representation plans.

Of those who are members of trade unions
- 6 hold office as president
- 5 " " " vice president
- 1 holds " " treasurer
- 3 hold " " secretary
- 9 " " " recording secretary
- 6 " " " trustee
- 1 holds " " business agent
- 3 hold " " organizer
- 3 " " " delegates to the central labor union
- 1 holds " " chairman shop committee
- 4 hold " " committeemen
- 1 holds " " financial secretary
- 3 hold " " members of executive board
- 1 holds " " division chairman

Of those who are members of company unions or employee representation plans
- 1 holds office as president
- 3 hold " " recording secretary
- 1 holds " " chairman
- 1 holds " " department representative

Forty-seven Pinkerton spies, or more than ⅓ of the total number in trade unions, according to their own list, hold office in the union. Is there any question that spy agencies are hired primarily for Union-Prevention and Union-Smashing?

In any case, of one thing we may be certain — employers who buy the service of the agencies know what they are paying for. And when the agency can't deliver the goods, or where workers are not organizing, then the service is discontinued. Corporations Auxiliary found that out. On July 6, 1936, one of its salesmen, D-H, wrote a letter to his head office telling of a conversation he had had with Mr. F. W. Marcolin, the Store Superintendent of the Bailey Company in Cleveland. Mr. Marcolin told him that the Bailey Company was going to discontinue the service of Corporations Auxiliary.

D-H asked him why "and he stated they did not think at the present time the expense was justified and the information they were receiving was not worth $200.00 a month. Said they had no complaint about the service but the operator had not gotten into the union and all the information he was able to gather covered daily routine. Some suggestions had been good but not worth the expense, also *there was apparently no union activity and they had decided to discontinue.*"

The Pinkerton agency met with a similar unhappy experience. They found that employers were not interested in their spy service unless they could take some action on the organizational activities of their workers. Mr. Meinbress, the superintendent of the San Francisco Pinkerton office, reported the sad news he had received from the general manager of the Western Pacific Railroad:

> Former client, friendly, said under the Eastman control *they cannot discharge for labor activities*, he knows pretty well who the agitators are but cannot help himself so *does not believe in spending money at present for secret work when he cannot act on the information.* I will keep up contact.
>
> J. C. MEINBRESS,
Official, San Francisco Office.

. . .

SENATOR LA FOLLETTE. Now apparently from this solicitor's report, while Mr. Eastman was coordinator, Mr. Meinbress found that under that situation employees of railroads are extended the same protection of the Wagner Labor Relations Act, since it extends to all employees, did he not, Mr. Pinkerton?

MR. PINKERTON. Yes, sir; it appears so.

SENATOR LA FOLLETTE. So it would appear from this superintendent's report that when your clients cannot discharge men for union activities, they have no use for your services, is that right?

MR. PINKERTON. I don't think that is always true; no, sir.

SENATOR LA FOLLETTE. I did not ask you if it was not always true. I asked you if it was not true.

MR. PINKERTON. It appears from this report to be true.

Had all employers of labor been as careful to obey the law as the general manager of the Western Pacific, then, in truth, the Pinkertons would have been in a bad way. But fortunately for the Pinkertons, this was not the case. Just as the Railway Labor Act extended protection to railway employees so the National Labor Relations Act (popularly known as the Wagner Act), extended that protection to other workers in July 1935. The intent of Congress in passing the Wagner Act is plain, the language is simple and easy to understand:

> Sec. 7. Employees shall have the right to self-organization, to form, join, or assist labor organizations, to bargain collectively through representatives of their own choosing, and to engage in concerted activities, for the purpose of collective bargaining or other mutual aid or protection.
>
> Sec. 8. It shall be an unfair labor practice for an employer —
>
> (1) To interfere with, restrain, or coerce employees in the exercise of the rights guaranteed in section 7.

It was a similar provision in the Railway Labor Act, plus the power of the strong railway unions, which kept the Western Pacific from hiring the Pinkertons. But many other employers throughout the country felt no such restraint. They did hire the Pinkertons and other agencies. And they did "interfere with, restrain, or coerce employees" in the exercise of their right to join unions. These employers were advised by eminent lawyers that they need not pay any attention to the Wagner Act because in their august opinion, the Act was unconstitutional. The National Committee of Lawyers of the American Liberty League, for example, took it upon itself to declare the Act unconstitutional. The Supreme Court of the United States, however, thought otherwise. On April 12, 1937 the Court declared the National Labor Relations Act constitutional. The 58 Liberty League Lawyers were in error.

One of the 5 cases that reached the Supreme Court in the Wagner Act decision was the Fruehauf Trailer Co. case. Unlike the Western Pacific, the management of this company felt that it did have the right (despite the Wagner Act) to discharge "agitators", i.e., union men. So it hired the Pinkerton agency to spy on its workers. The Pinkertons obliged. On complaint of the union, the members of the National Labor Relations Board examined the evidence and came to this conclusion: "The Board found that the workers had been discharged because of their union activity and that the company's policy was to disrupt the local of the United Automobile Workers Federal Labor Union and so to defeat collective bargaining."

How was this done? Excerpts from the Board report show the steps. First, Martin, a Pinkerton spy is given employment in the plant. "He thereafter joined the union and eventually became its treasurer. He was thus able to procure a list of all the members of the union. He made reports more than once a week to the respondent [Fruehauf Trailer Co.], and the lists of members which he furnished were given to the respondent's superintendent, Halpin. With these lists in his hand Halpin went about the factory from time to time and warned various employees against union activities. The result of Martin's activities caused suspicion, unrest, and confusion among the employees . . . Completely armed by Martin with the necessary information the respondent determined to put a stop to all attempts on the part of its factory workers to form an efficient independent bargaining agency, and in furtherance of that purpose summarily discharged nine men and threatened three others with discharge . . . As to the discharges we find: Nicholas Trusch was employed as a carpenter in the body shop of the respondent for five and a half years and had a good record, no fault ever having been found with his work or conduct. His foreman, Rosenbusch, asked him on July 15, 1935, 'Do you want your job or your union?' When Trusch replied that he would not give up the union he was discharged between 9 and 10 in the morning of the same day . . . We find that Trusch was discharged for the reason that he joined and assisted the union." The Board takes up the cases of the nine men, one by one, and its closing sentence is the same every time, "discharged for the reason that he joined and assisted the union." Here in graphic detail, in this N.L.R.B. report, is the story of industrial espionage.

Not the whole story, however. There's one other angle. The discharged men can find no other jobs — they are blacklisted everywhere, because they dared to join the union. They are thrown on the public relief rolls. Let Mr. Edwin S. Smith, member of the N.L.R.B. appointed by the President, tell the tale: "I have never listened to anything more tragically un-American than stories of the discharged employees of the Fruehauf Trailer Co., victims of a labor spy. Man after man in the prime of life, of obvious character and courage, came before us to tell of the blows that had fallen on him for his crime of having joined a union. Here they were — family men with wives and children — on public relief, blacklisted from employment, so they claimed, in the city of Detroit, citizens whose only offense was that they had ventured in the land of the free to organize as employees to improve their working conditions. Their reward, as workers who had given their best to their employer, was to be hunted down by a hired spy like the lowest of criminals and thereafter tossed like useless metal on the scrap heap."

You can see from the tone of his testimony that Mr. Smith is angry because he thinks an injustice was done. He was disturbed, too, because he saw in labor espionage a danger to our democratic institutions. He said as much at this hearing in April 1936. That was before the sit-down strike at General Motors and Chrysler occurred, and it should be full of meaning to those people who cannot understand why American workers have become so militant. Here is Mr. Smith's warning, "The aims of one group may be cordially detested by another, but for the stronger group to suppress the minority's right to express its opinion is to suppress democracy itself. Those who would encroach upon the civil liberties of any group are playing with dangerous and destructive fire. Democracy may be attacked from the right as well as from the left. The denial of civil liberties is itself an important step toward revolution."

It's a familiar and oft-repeated story — this suppression by the stronger group, of the workers' right to organize. In Duquesne, in 1919, the minute any labor organizers stepped into the town they were clapped into jail. The mayor there boasted that no union could hold a meeting in Duquesne even if Jesus Christ were the organizer. And in Homestead, in 1933, Secretary of Labor Perkins found that the streets and parks and halls were closed to her — the only place she could meet with a committee of steel workers was in the U. S. Post Office! This sort of thing is still true in many parts of the United States in 1937 — in spite of the Wagner Act. Unfortunately we cannot devote adequate space in these pages to these open violations of the workers' right to organize. Here we are concerned with the undercover violations, the wrecking of unions through the use of spies, as in the Fruehauf Trailer Co. case.

You can easily imagine what the effect of industrial espionage has been on the workers. They don't have to read about stool-pigeons to know about them — they know about them from sad experience. It is for that reason that many of them who see the necessity for joining a union, hesitate to do so. They are afraid. George A. Patterson, a steel worker, told the committee, "that there is an espionage system in the steel plants . . . is common talk amongst the employees at all times. They know it, and they feel it. They feel that at all times they are being watched. As we have tried to organize, many a man would say 'We would like to come in, but it is just as much as our job is worth to join up.' They have said that many times. I can say that they are truthful in their opinion about that, because when we go around with the applications and ask the men to come into the organization they talk about stool-pigeons, and so on."

Only through organization into unions can the workers protect their own interests. When N.I.R.A. gave them this right in 1933, the employers fell back on an old scheme to take the teeth out of such organizations. "The men have a right to organize? O.K. Let them organize. We will even help them — we'll give them a plan for organization and put up the money to foot the bill. We'll back the men to the limit in forming unions — company unions."

It was truly amazing with what speed company unions sprang into existence in industries hitherto unorganized. N.I.R.A. was passed June 16, 1933. Before the end of the month plans for the formation of company unions were announced in the plants of U. S. Steel, Republic Steel, Weirton Steel, and Jones and Laughlin. The automobile industry showed the same lightning-like speed in the organization of company unions. The N.R.A. code in autos was approved on August 27, 1933. Ten days before, Chevrolet, Buick, Fisher Body and other General Motors subsidiaries had perfected their "representation" plans; the Chrysler Corporation followed in October.

From all this undue haste, and from the fact that the employers were behind the company union plans, it becomes obvious even to people inexperienced in labor matters, that there must be something fishy about company unions. There is. In a study called "The Economics of the Iron and Steel Industry," financed jointly by the Brookings Institution and the Falk Foundation, one sentence gives the whole show away: "The evidence shows conclusively that the great majority of the plans (company unions) were favored and fostered by the companies in order *to forestall outside unionization.*" The cat's out of the bag. Here is the reason why some of the steel companies have been paying out a quarter of a million dollars every year to finance their company unions.

Company unions have been set up "to forestall outside unionization." But, as we have seen, Union-Prevention is part of the province of the private detective agencies. Are they left out in the cold? Not on your life. They are specialists in every kind of Union-Prevention. If it's company unions that are necessary to do the trick, they are prepared to make that part of their service. Thus the Butler System of Industrial Survey, New York, advises prospective clients, "Where it is desired that company unions be formed we first sell the idea to the workers and thereafter promote its development into completion. Hundreds of such organizations have been formed by us to date."

Was the Butler System alone in the field? It was not. Railway Audit, we learn from one of their letters placed in evidence, knew all of the tricks of the company union game. Mr. L. D. Rice, vice president and general manager, gives a few pointers to Mr. W. H. Gray who is out in the field soliciting business. "We have been successful in assisting in starting a lot of employees' associations, and I think that you will find some of the manufacturers interested along this line. At the present time the non-union employees of Reading, Pa., get out a semi-monthly paper, and it is a mighty good one. It combats the union paper. Quite often they expose some of the things that the unions do. No doubt Mr. Ivey has a copy in Atlanta, and I am requesting him to send you one so that you can look over it.

"Some of our people are very instrumental in assisting in the publication of this paper, as well as the entertainment, etc. that these non-union employees carry on.

"You can also start the same kind of organizations in other textile plants."

This branch of the agencies' service — the setting up of company unions — was a good talking point when business was bad, i.e., where there was no "labor trouble." On those occasions spy agencies became "insurance salesmen," according to A. E. Lawson, formerly secretary of the National Corporation Service. Here is Mr. Lawson on the witness stand:

> SENATOR LA FOLLETTE. Now, when there were not any labor troubles, can you tell us how you got business then?
>
> MR. LAWSON. Well, we sold the business on a proposition of business insurance, "Protect yourself and find out what is going on in your plant before trouble actually does occur."
>
> SENATOR LA FOLLETTE. Did you ever have occasions where the client would be assured in a situation of that kind that something could be done in the way of helping to build up company unions?

MR. LAWSON. Yes, I know of such cases . . . We put men in the Newton Steel Company at Newton Falls just after the plant was reopened for business and formed a company union there. We also formed a company union in the Taylor Winfield Company at Warren, Ohio, *to offset any possibility of joining the outside union.*

SENATOR LA FOLLETTE. How did they go about setting up these company unions, if you know?

MR. LAWSON. Well, they would put one man in as a leader, furnish him with information as to bylaws and regulations of the company union.

SENATOR LA FOLLETTE. Who usually prepared the bylaws, and so forth?

MR. LAWSON. Well, we had probably 15 or 20 different set-ups from other manufacturing plants.

SENATOR LA FOLLETTE. You would sell the client the one he liked best?

MR. LAWSON. We would sell him the one that we thought would fit the plant best.

SENATOR LA FOLLETTE. You usually got his approval of it before you started up?

MR. LAWSON. Oh, certainly.

(That does have a familiar ring, doesn't it? "Do you want an endowment policy, a 20-year-life, or an annuity? We are prepared to sell you exactly the kind of insurance that is best suited to your needs.")

One other point needs to be cleared up. How were the workers in the plants persuaded to throw in their lot with the company union? In many plants they had no choice — it was a case of join the company union or lose your job. But in some plants where the workers inclined toward their own union, what arguments were used to swing them into the company union? Mr. C. M. Kuhl, an operative of fourteen years experience with several agencies, answers that question. "These inside operators would talk and talk against the union, the American Federation of Labor, and use a point similar to this, 'Well why pay dues to a lot of organizers, presidents, secretaries . . . ?'

"And another, 'For instance, if we give a dollar here in our particular local only a quarter stays here, and so much goes down to Columbus at the State headquarters and the rest goes to Washington. So out of an actual dollar we put in the American Federation of Labor union why we only keep that quarter here. Now, if we keep a company union we don't pay any dues, and we save those dues, which will amount to $2 or $3 a month.'"

There is little doubt that these were effective arguments. The growth of company unions after 1933 was tremendous. And spy agencies played a great part in their formation.

But the growth of legitimate trade unions after 1933 was also tremendous. This happened in spite of the poisonous activities of the spy agencies, which were so active in Union-Prevention and Union-Smashing. American labor after 1933 was on the march and trade unions were bound to gain strength in the face of any opposition, no matter how powerful. But had it not been for the undercover activities of the detective agencies, they would have grown even stronger. Of that there is no doubt. Senator La Follette listened to the evidence for weeks. He was chairman of the committee that conducted the inquiry. He is in a position to know. Here is his opinion: "In the light of the testimony this committee has taken, the evidence is overwhelming, in the opinion of the chairman of this committee, that the injection of these labor spies in the unions, and the fact that they come to be in charge of union activities, get to be officers of unions, cart those records back and forth to the detective agency offices, report the names of men who apply for membership to the management of corporations, have demonstrated beyond any doubt in the minds of any fair-minded persons whatsoever, that the use of this labor espionage is demonstrated and proved to be one of the most effective weapons in destroying genuine labor collective bargaining activities on the part of workers."

III. Spies at Work

SO MUCH FOR what the agencies do. Now how do they do it? What is the technique for Union-Prevention and Union-Smashing?

Let's begin with the spy. He may be brought into the factory from the outside and given a job, as Martin, the Pinkerton spy, was brought into the Fruehauf Trailer plant. Or he may be one of the men already at work in the plant, who is persuaded or tricked into becoming a spy. (How that is done is a long and interesting story which will be told in the next chapter.) But in either case, whether he is an outside operative brought into the plant, or one of the workers already there, he does his day's work at the bench or on the belt just as the other workmen do. Few people in the plant know who he is — maybe only the plant superintendent or the personnel director. The foreman seldom knows. The workers seldom know. For the stool-pigeon is one of them — a worker. He eats with them, talks as they do, complains about the same injustices, goes out with them at night to the movies or to the union meetings. The workers know only that they are being spied on, but who the spy is they don't know. After they find out, if they ever do, then of course it's easy to think back to a hundred and one little incidents which should have made them suspicious; but before they find out it's not so easy — very often the exposed stool-pigeon is the man whom they would have least suspected.

It's the spy's job to make friends with as many workers as possible, win their confidence, and listen to their talk. He must keep his eyes and ears open at all times — and report what he sees and hears. Here are the specific instructions of the Railway Audit & Inspection Co. to one of its operatives in a knitting mill:

34

While working in this plant it will be necessary that you do whatever work you are assigned in such a manner as to be pleasing to all concerned and not cause you to be laid off or discharged for not carrying out such orders as are given you . . .

It will be necessary that you mingle with the employees so that you can win their confidence to such an extent that the men will confide in you and will inform you as to just what they are doing, etc.

It will be necessary that you render a good, detailed, lengthy report each and every day covering conditions as you find them, reporting in detail the conversations you hold, those you over-hear, etc., and try to make each day's work just a little more interesting than the day's report before, and we feel sure if you will be observant to all that is going on around you, you will be able to report many things of value to this client and will be kept working there indefinitely.

You are to mail your reports promptly to the writer, to Mr. W. A. Schraisen, post office box 793, Philadelphia, Pa. Do not hold up your reports and mail them in a couple at a time, but let them come in promptly each day, so that the client will receive the information before it is too old.

Report on conditions as you find them, also offer any suggestions you feel will be of value to the client — be on the alert for what is taking place, report all you possibly can learn regarding the attitude toward the company, their immediate superiors, one another, etc. — whether there is any union agitation, etc., any loafing, stealing, waste of time, materials, etc., how they do their work, the good as well as the bad. On Sundays and when not working in the plant it will be necessary that you render a report, and in order to do so, so that the client can be billed for the day, it will be essential that you associate with some of the employees outside, i.e., get out among them, visit them, so that they will be able to obtain from some of the employees information that you may be able to secure in no other way for much information of value to the client is gained in this way.

Therefore, it is essential that you make as many contacts as you possibly can, so as to be able to cover as much ground as you can possibly do, meet some of the employees on your way to work, in the mornings, also during lunch hour, and on your way home in the evenings, as well as by making appointments to meet some of them in the evenings in order to become better acquainted with them. This you will not be able to do all at once, but you will gradually work up to this as you become better acquainted with the various employees, and it is desired that you start out the first few days easy and not be too forward, so as to win the confidence of the employees and be able to continue indefinitely.

The usual practice is for the spy to write a daily report, sign it with his code number, put it in an envelope without a return address, and mail it to a post office box in the city where the agency official who is in charge of that particular job is located.

The post office box is not rented in the real name of the agency or of any of its operatives. It is rented under a fake name. The spy report is picked up each day, brought to the agency office and read by the agency official who is handling that job. This official then edits the report. He corrects the spelling and the grammar, eliminates the irrelevant material, and fixes up the report in general. Sometimes he really fixes it up — not only subtracts unimportant details from the original, but also *adds* important — and untrue — details to the original. Next, the edited report is typed and sent to the client.

Then what? The axe falls. Before long, the manager may be called into the superintendent's office and told to discharge John Smith, Joe Brown, and several others. "But why?" protests the manager. "Smith is one of my best workers, and Brown is steady and reliable, he's worked here for seven years. And there's nothing wrong with the other boys you want me to fire. What's it all about?"

"You're wrong, sir, there is something wrong with all these men. They're agitators. They're talking union to the men. We can't have that here. They must go," replies the superintendent. "And — er — be sure you don't tell them why you're firing them. Think up some excuse — drunkenness, or being late, or wasting materials — anything. But get rid of them."

Now let's look at the successive steps:

SPY REPORT EN ROUTE

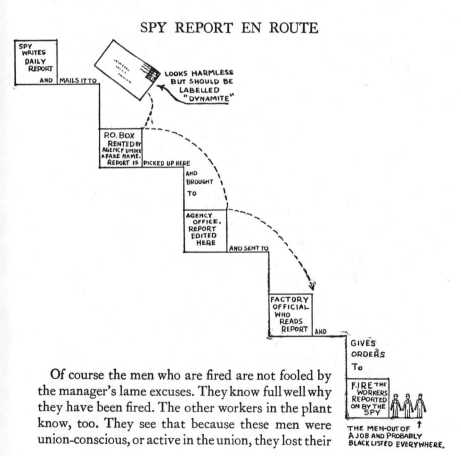

Of course the men who are fired are not fooled by the manager's lame excuses. They know full well why they have been fired. The other workers in the plant know, too. They see that because these men were union-conscious, or active in the union, they lost their jobs. Naturally, these other workers are afraid. When the union organizer tries to interest them in the union, they shy away. The baby union is smothered in infancy. Or, if the workers are already members of the union, they turn up less frequently at meetings — and after a while, they drop out. The grown-up union is strangled. The spy has done his job.

Not all of it, however. So far his job has been easy. But he has other work to do. And this other work is more difficult. Where there is a union, he must get into it and make it ineffective, cause dissension, break it up if possible. That's harder. But it is done. Remember the Flint local of 22,000 in 1935 which slid down to 122 in 1936; remember Roszel who was able in Hartford, to force a membership of 2500 down to 75. Exactly how is it done — how does the spy go about sabotaging the union?

We get a clue from part of a spy report of a union meeting:

Erie, Nov. 17th, 1933.

Local No. 101. I. A. of M., met at C. L. U. Hall, 1703 State at Friday evening.

Meeting called to order promptly at 8 P.M., President C Hall presiding, Financial Sec'y Henry Searle, also present. (These two men both work at the Standard Stoker.)

Seven members in attendance.

Communication from grand lodge, acknowledging receipt of letter from local #101, addressed to Mr. Brown of Cleveland, and who is organizer from this district, and asking the grand lodge to furnish an organizer for Erie, grand lodge stated the matter was rec'g attention and would answer later.

No new applications, no initiations.

[It was] Suggested that a comm't'ee of three out of work members be appointed to act as an organizing com't'ee and look up several men who had paid in sums of .25 cts to $2. on applications and had not been heard from since. This com't'ee was to go out and look these men up and also try to see other

machinists and get them to join the union and to pay their
own expenses and serve without pay.

This was called absurd by Shults, who said if those who
were working were not interested enough in trying to better
their conditions . . . it was absurd to think that out of work
members were going to spend time and money trying to organize, this and the fact that the grand lodge was thinking
the matter over of giving Erie some help in organizing work,
some of the other members then spoke along the same lines
and criticized the grand lodge for not getting on the job and
the matter was allowed to drop, no action taken . . .

D. G.

Here we see the cunning spy carrying on his destructive work inside the union. Follow the steps. One of the members has a good
idea. Some of the unionists are out of work — nothing to do, and
lots of free time. Let three of them act as a committee whose job it
shall be to bring more members into the union. Let them begin by
rounding up those machinists who have already filed their applications to join, and have even paid in some money. Obviously all that
these workers need is just one more push and they'll be in the
union. Next, let the committee go after other machinists and try to
get them to join. It's a good idea because if the committee is successful the union will have been strengthened with the addition of new
members; if the committee is unsuccessful, nothing is lost, since the
members of the committee were idle anyway.

Now what happens? Up hops Shults who calls the plan "absurd."
When he is through talking, not only is the matter "*allowed to drop,
no action taken,*" but some of the members *have been led to criticize
"the grand lodge for not getting on the job.*" Net result: plan for increasing membership — spiked; also, dissatisfaction with the
grand lodge instilled in the minds of several members. A good
night's work — for anyone interested in hurting, not helping the
union.

Who is responsible? Shults is responsible, according to the report of D. G., the code initial of the spy. But is Shults also a spy? He is. Shults is D. G., and D. G. is Shults. They are one and the same. When D. G. here reports on the fine wrecking job done by Shults, he is boasting about his own exploits.

Now let us attend another meeting of the machinists' local in Erie, two weeks later. With the help of the report of D. G. (Shults) we can see what happens:

Erie, Dec. 1st, 1933.

Meeting Called to Order by President Hall with eleven members present . . .

The new officers for the coming year were elected no great change in personnel, and some of the newly elected men have not been members a year, the constitution of the machinist calls for a membership of one year before eligible to hold office, but the new members looked harmless so thought best not to object.

Federal Local organizer, Winters, had requested some of the members to let him come in and explain his pet scheme of taking all machinist into the Federal Local then telling them that they must join the machinist Union; the member who proposed his coming in stated that Winters advised that his organizing of the Olacker Mfg. Co. was being held up because the machinist at this plant refused to pay in $5.00 to join the Machinist Union while it only cost the rest 2.00 to join the Federal Local, and unless he could take the machinist in at 2.00 he (Winters) couldn't organize the plant. Several members seemed to think it was all right, but after some discussion a member (Shults) took the floor and objected to allowing the man to enter, told them his scheme was unconstitutional and that he knew it, that the members of this Machinist Local ought to know if they read the constitution and that any man who wanted to join a trade and didn't think it was worth 5.00 to belong probably wouldn't amount to much as a member, and would probably expect the Local to help him get a raise the first week he belonged, that the thing to do was to settle it once and for all. Tell Mr. Winters that machinist must join the machinist local or else they couldn't join anything in Erie, this action was taken and Winters was denied the Floor.

Nothing else of interest transpired . . .

D. G.

Thus Shults, the spy, "settles it once and for all." The union organizer has trouble enrolling new members because the initial fee is too high; he has a plan to get over this difficulty which he wants to explain to the local. But Shults is on the job. He is interested in preventing organization. He defeats the plan by pointing out that it is unconstitutional. Result? "Winters was denied the Floor."

Notice that Shults is really no stickler for the constitution. He uses it only where he needs to. He points out that several of the newly elected officers of the union have been elected contrary to the provisions of the constitution — but he doesn't object because "the new members looked harmless."

Everything under control — Shults's control. A few more meetings like these two with Shults squelching every proposed scheme for getting new members, and soon there won't be any members at all. The union will be dead.

The technique is plain. Shults is obviously bright. He knows how to talk. He gives plausible arguments. He is ever on the watch — against the interests of the union. And he has applied himself to the task. How many members of a union ever bother really to learn the constitution? Very few. The spy does — it's part of his technique of destruction. How many members of a union ever try to become an officer in the union? Very few. Most workers are shy, or modest, or haven't time. Not so the spy. He has the agency's orders to do just that — to become an officer in the union. How many members of a union care to, or dare to, serve on committees in the union? Very few. The spy does — it's an important part of his technique of de-

struction. Most union members are quite content to let the other
fellow do the talking and the working — they prefer to play a pas-
sive role. But the spy has no choice — to do his best work, he must
play an active role. Most workers do not consider that it is *their job
to build up and strengthen their union;* but the spy knows that it is
his job to tear down and weaken the union. And there's where the spy
has the edge over the honest trade unionists.

Let's watch another spy at work. This time the story is contained
in the sworn affidavit of Charles Killinger, an automobile union
organizer from Michigan:

> I, Charles Killinger, being duly sworn, deposes and says:
> I have been an active member of the union for the last three
> years and am at present a part-time organizer for the union.
> John Stott was on the legislative committee of the Amalga-
> mated Local #156 and was also chairman of the Welfare com-
> mittee. Chairmanship of the welfare committee gave him an
> opportunity to visit a number of union people who were sick
> at various times. He visited me some months ago when I was
> ill, and after consoling with me about my illness, began to
> abuse the work being done by Wyndham Mortimer and Rob-
> ert Travis, the international organizers who had been sent into
> Flint during the summer. The executive board of the Local
> #156 was particularly quiescent as far as organization went and
> it was the unceasing work of Mortimer and then of Travis
> which led to the building up of the union. This was apparent to
> everyone but bothered a number of individuals who seemed to
> delight in keeping the union as small as possible. On the occa-
> sion of his visit to me, Stott said about Mortimer and Travis,
> "They are no good. They don't do any work . . . When we
> get rid of Mortimer and Travis we will be able to do something
> here" . . .

Stott was always very active on the floor of the meetings,
took part in all discussions, but always managed to raise hair-
splitting questions on motions before the assembly, tending to

confuse many of the younger members and to check decisive action by the union.

CHARLES KILLINGER

Spy Stott's technique is clear from this affidavit. In the last paragraph, we find him using tactics similar to those employed by Shults, raising "hair-splitting questions tending to confuse many of the younger members and to check decisive action by the union." Anyone who has ever attended a meeting in which endless time is spent in debating hair-splitting questions knows how very annoying that can be. If it happens at every meeting — and Shults and Stott were there to make it happen — then many of the members begin to look upon union meetings as a bore to be avoided if possible, which is exactly what the spies want to accomplish.

Equally annoying, if not more so, is belonging to an organization which sets up committees to perform certain tasks which somehow never get done. The spy knows this and frequently worms his way on to as many committees as possible with the sole purpose of sabotaging their work. We learn from Killinger's affidavit that Stott, the spy, was on both the legislative and the welfare committees. We learn from another affidavit, that of Walter Reed, active union member of Local #156, that Stott was also elected secretary of the negotiating or grievance committee. How did he perform his duties on that important committee? Reed tells us:

The committee didn't function in spite of the fact that there were cases to be taken up. October, 1936 we had a meeting of the Chevrolet unit called by Robert Travis for the purpose of discussing what grievances they should take up before the management. The negotiating committee was very insistent that they should not go down because they had no grievances. We said that we had general grievances that should be taken up, such as seniority rights, shop conditions, and hours. The committee said they wanted individual grievances, signed, and said that was all they could handle. Even though there were some men with personal grievances, the committee refused, and Stott made a speech saying that these men should not go down to the management, *so nothing was done about it.*

What will be the temper of those men with grievances who go to the committee set up by the union to handle their cases when they find the committee will do nothing for them? The spy knows that this "nothing was done about it" is a very effective way of causing dissatisfaction. Equally effective is Stott's other tactic as chairman of the welfare committee, that of visiting the members and buzzing into their ears criticisms of the leadership. Now it is true that the leadership of many unions is not above criticism. Often the leadership is stupid, self-satisfied, inactive — asleep at the switch. Such leadership should, of course, be criticized severely. But the spy is not concerned with legitimate criticism where it is truly justified. He criticizes all leadership but his own — one more tactic in his arsenal of weapons against unions.

We see this clearly in the activity of another spy, Francis Arthur Roszel. We have met the worthy Mr. Roszel before. In 1935, you remember, he was secretary of a local in Hartford which he succeeded in smashing. He was the spy who answered the questionnaire on dick agencies sent out by the A. F. of L. He was exposed — and one year later he turns up again as a member of a local of the United Automobile Workers in Michigan! Here he continues his activity as stool-pigeon and union-smasher. Part of another sworn affidavit shows Roszel at work:

> The union organizer connected with the local union at this plant was and is Stanley Novak. Novak is a Pole. Roszel continually agitated the members of the union against "foreign", and Polish leadership in the union, with the quite apparent objective of creating dissension and causing Novak to be discredited.
>
> Notwithstanding the fact that Roszel went on the picket line from time to time during the strike, he continually agitated among the men, urging them to go back to work. His line was that the strike had been called by a mere handful of men, that

the members of the Union had not been consulted, etc. Here again was an attack upon the leadership and an effort to break the strike.

Shults, Stott, and Roszel were evidently able hard-working spies, well versed in the tactics best suited to Union-Smashing. Now try to imagine a man who combines all the "virtues" of all three of them and you have a picture of Bart Furey, a spy planted in the Electric Auto-Lite Company of Toledo in 1934. Furey was Shults, Stott, and Roszel all rolled into one. Like Shults, he was familiar with the constitution and parliamentary procedure; in addition, "He knew the international rules; he even knew the international officers . . . He knew them personally, man to man, all the international executive officers." Like Stott, he "handled" the grievances of the men, i.e., he did nothing about them. "It seemed as if he would go so far but he would not go out of his road to help these boys on their grievances . . . the grievances would pile up." Like Roszel in Hartford, Furey became an officer in the union — first, chairman of the executive shop committee, and later president of the union; like Roszel in Michigan, Furey attacked the leadership — witness this sworn affidavit by Edith Roberts:

> I had been very active in the union, and was one of the leaders among the girls. I was on the various committees of the union. But after refusing this offer [Furey asked Miss Roberts to become a spy] Furey got after me in the union and told the others he didn't want me on any of the committees of the union. He told people not to vote for me, saying to several that she should not be put on the committee otherwise he would not serve as chairman since "she was too dumb, she blocks everything I try to put across." He went even further than that, asking various people around the shop to sign a petition to have me ousted from my job in the shop.
>
> I told the story of his offer to me to several people in the union, but he had them so wrapped around his finger that no one would believe the story. On two different occasions after

the conversation with him and my refusal of the offer, I have received anonymous letters which were put under my door telling me to keep my mouth shut . . . I am and was an active militant union leader among the women in the shop and was constantly trying to bring the women forward in the union. Furey did everything he could to get me removed from any position of influence, after I had turned down his offer.

Also in the record, is another affidavit, by Homer Martin, concerning Furey's many attempts to split up Local 12; and his endeavor "in every way possible to write such provisions into the International Constitution as would completely emasculate the International Union and create a loosely-federated group of local unions. This move by Furey was only defeated because of the staunchness of the other members of that committee."

A very busy spy was Mr. Bart Furey. Let it be said of him, in all fairness, that he failed in the end, not because of his own weakness, but because of the strength of some of the union members; not because he did not take seriously his job of Union-Smashing, but because opposed to him were some workers who took seriously their job of Union-Building.

Still another tactic for Union-Smashing is that of robbing the treasury. Too many one-time members of unions have lost faith in trade unionism because the treasurer of their local ran off with the money. Very often that treasurer is a spy. In this connection, two affidavits are in the record concerning the activities of Richard Adlen, a spy. "Adlen was . . . always prominent in handling social affairs and on several occasions wormed his way into a position in the union where he could handle the finances. He has on a number of occasions been accused of misappropriating funds or not properly accounting for funds entrusted to him by the union . . . Adlen was a part of a committee that handled the finances for a big labor day picnic in 1934. They were alleged to have made a profit of $1200.00 and we never could get hold of the accounts. It was investigated by the union, but only $1.49 was turned in."

Spies are on to the fact that it doesn't take more than one or two such raids on the union treasury before unions of several thousand members are shaken down to a handful. Spies are also on to the fact that while the strike is a useful effective trade-union weapon, an ill-advised and ill-timed strike is dangerous for a union — so they do what they can to start such strikes. Spies are on to the fact that for union officials to conclude a sell-out agreement with an employer destroys the morale of the union members — so they do what they can to effect such agreements. Spies are on to any and every method of Union-Smashing and Union-Prevention. They do all they can to make use of those methods.

No recital of spy activities along these lines is complete without the story of Louis Foster who single-handed, it appears, was able to forestall the unionization of thousands of workers. This story is in the record. It is sworn to by John D. Lengel, for eight years the business agent for the International Association of Machinists in the northern New Jersey area. Here is part of Mr. Lengel's account of the activities of spy Louis Foster:

In about May 1934, Louis Foster, without any solicitation on the part of the union, [local #340, Newark, N. J.], applied for membership in that local. He stated that he was, at that time, working in the Worthington Pump Company at Harrison, New Jersey.

Louis Foster immediately became a very active union member. He volunteered for work on all Committees and took a very active part in discussions on the floor during the meetings of the local. He was a very intelligent and able speaker and was recognized by the men as having some of the qualities of leadership.

He volunteered for work on the Entertainment Committee to raise funds for the union. This job involved a lot of work and time on the part of the member who took the responsibility. *Foster stated that he wanted the roster of members of the local in order to send out invitations to the entertainment for the purpose of raising money for the lodge. The roster was turned over to him.*

A year later I discovered that the manufacturers in the vicinity had a complete list of the members of local #340, as of March 1935. This was the same list that had been turned over to Foster and could have only been secured through him.

During this year *Foster volunteered to be the representative from the machinists union to the convention of the New Jersey State Federation of Labor.* This position involves personal expenses on the part of the member who volunteers, but Foster was willing to assume the expense and the time involved.

The Union, local #340, was having great difficulty in securing new members. The reason being that the machinists in this area were of the opinion that they could not be protected in their jobs if they joined the union. *It was common knowledge that the manufacturers were able to find out which employees had signed applications in the union and thus discharged them.* In and about September 1935, I held a meeting of the employees of the Lionel Manufacturing Company of Irvington, New Jersey. The meeting was held at the Labor Lyceum in Newark. *Foster was present at that meeting and took a very active part in it.* About 120 employees attended the meeting out of which about 30 signed applications giving their names and addresses. *About two days after the meeting, approximately 26 out of the 30 who had given their names and addresses were discharged. Foster had access to the applications and no doubt turned them over to the employer.*

During this year *Foster succeeded in being elected as representative from the lodge to the District Council of Machinists.* About this time there appeared to be *a good deal of internal disputes within the union.* One group in the union contended that I was not properly fulfilling my duties as business agent and was not succeeding in getting many new members. Foster took the leadership of this faction which attempted to oust me as business agent . . . However, I was elected. Later in the year, despite the fact that Foster had been claiming that I was getting too much salary and it ought to be reduced, *he made a mo-*

*tion on the floor that I be presented with $100.00 Christmas bonus
and a new car. This manoeuver on his part caused considerable
confusion and dissatisfaction in the union.*

In the early part of 1936, the union started a campaign to
organize the machinists in the automobile repair companies in
Newark. At our first organizational meeting we had a large
crowd of enthusiastic prospective members. *Within a few weeks
every company in which we were able to secure applications, got
information as to which of their employees had signed with the
union and there were wholesale discharges . . .*

I have recently discovered that Louis Foster has been in the
employ of the manufacturers in the vicinity by virtue of his
employment as a spy for the International Auxiliary Corporation. It is now clear to me that *he has been responsible for the
prevention of organization in my territory; that he has been a destructive force in the union; that he prevented the real organization
for collective bargaining of the 20,000 employees* who are eligible
for membership in my territory.

Just look back over the italicized parts of that quotation. Some
of those activities might be indulged in by any honest union member. Some of them only a spy would engage in. Take them altogether
and you have almost a perfect picture of the spy technique of
Union-Prevention and Union-Smashing.

IV. The Gentle Art of Hooking

ANDREWS . . . Letteer . . . Martin . . . Shults . . . Stott
. . . Roszel . . . Furey . . . Foster . . . and a host of others —
all spies. Capable, energetic men, some of them with real qualities
of leadership — all stool-pigeons Why? What happened to these
competent shrewd men and the thousands of others like them,
which inclined them toward a career of betrayal of their fellow-
workers?

Some were inclined that way to begin with and welcomed the
opportunity to pick up easy money. Others were unfortunate — they
had the bad luck of being so placed that they could be of service to
the spy agencies. It may have been because of the very fact that
they were so smart; it may have been because they held key positions in the union; it may have been only because they happened
to be working in a particular department in a factory. Whatever
the reason, they were in a position where they could be of use to the
agency. They were needed for a special job.

So they were "hooked."

"Hooking" is the technical term for the conversion, by an agency
operative, of an honest workman into a spy. How is it done?

Mr. Williams, a worker, comes home some night to find a stranger
in his house waiting for him. The stranger, an affable, courteous
gentleman, says he represents a group of the stockholders who are
interested in finding out whether the plant is being run as efficiently
as possible, whether the management is fair to the men, etc. Would
Mr. Williams be interested in supplying this information which
would be of great use to the stockholders and would harm nobody?
Of course, the stockholders would pay him for his trouble — say $15
a week for writing a daily report. Mr. Williams, unsuspecting and

in need of the extra money, agrees. He understands that secrecy will be necessary because the stockholders do not want to act upon their findings until they have collected all the facts. So he consents to write a daily report to a box number in another city. He is paid $15 in cash in advance for the first week and he signs a receipt. All is well.

But not for long. Another week or two goes by and then the stranger in another visit, suggests that he's slipping — his work isn't as good as it should be. "We want more of what the men are talking about, any complaints they have, any union activity, etc." At this point, Mr. Williams may become suspicious and balk at the idea. He may then be persuaded that clearly he would be doing no wrong if he wrote his reports as suggested because all that the stockholders are interested in is tracking down the Communists, agitators, and troublemakers. So he continues, making his reports "better," as suggested. The extra money comes in handy all this while so that when he finally realizes that he has become a paid stool-pigeon it's hard for him to give it up. He is "hooked."

If, however, he realizes earlier that there is something shady about the whole business and decides to quit, he may be gently reminded that he has been receiving money for spying, and what would his fellow workers think of him when they are shown his signed receipts? A strong man faced with this possibility decides to come clean anyway, tell his fellow workers he has been framed, and see what happens. A weak man is frightened — and remains "hooked." He works in the plant as before, draws his usual wages as a workman, and writes daily spy reports on the activities of his friends in the factory.

The record of the La Follette committee hearings is studded with cases of such hooking of innocent men. Even the agency heads admitted it was a common practice with them (though some of them had an aversion to the term "hooking" — they preferred to say "employing" or "making contact with"). Mr. Kuhl, the operative with 14 years experience who knows every angle of the business, was a willing witness — he had decided to quit the business. Here is the record of his testimony on hooking:

SENATOR LA FOLLETTE. Have you ever done any hooking or roping?

MR. KUHL. Yes, sir.

SENATOR LA FOLLETTE. How do you do that?

MR. KUHL. Well, first you look your prospect over, and if he is married that is preferable. If he is financially hard up, that is number two. If his wife wants more money or he hasn't got a car, that all counts. And you go offer him this extra money, naturally you don't tell him what you want him for. You have got some story that you are representing some bankers or some bondholders or an insurance company and they want to know what goes on in there.   · · ·

SENATOR LA FOLLETTE. After a fellow gets hooked suppose he wants to get unhooked; is that difficult for him?

MR. KUHL. Well, if he is a good man and you don't want to lose him, because they are hard to hook, you will try to keep him with you. You have his receipts, and probably he will sign a receipt with a number, and he says "Aw, hell, that don't mean anything. That is only a number." But still you have his handwriting where he wrote in his original reports.

Once hooked, it becomes the operative's next job to get himself elected to some office in the union so he can have ready access to the names of the members — to be reported to the agency — to be reported to the firm — to be discharged. Roy Williams was one such operative. Here is his affidavit:

I, Roy Williams, of my own free will do voluntarily acknowledge I have been in the employ of the Corporations Auxiliary Corporation as espionage operative and at the same time and during the same period I was the elected and active Recording Secy. & Trustee of the Graham-Paige local of the United Automobile Workers.   Signed: ROY WILLIAMS

Witness: EDWARD AYERS
RICHARD T. FRANKENSTEEN
L. S. GROGAN

Richard Frankensteen, one of the witnesses to this confession, has now become a member of the executive board of the United Automobile Workers. In his testimony to the La Follette committee, he made the following statement about Mr. Williams. "He was, I believe, the best liked and most popular man in Graham-Paige Motor Company. He worked there for 17 years. He was very well thought of. He was elected to the position of recording secretary, and this year is chairman of the board of trustees. He had worked there for 17 years and only during the last 3 years has he been hired by the Corporations Auxiliary. He was hooked into it. By that I mean they got him in; they roped him. He did not know what it was about until they got him in. Then when he tried to get out I understand that a Mr. H. L. Madison urged him to stay in — told him his work was perfectly all right, that he should stay, there was nothing wrong, that the Corporations Auxiliary was not the same type as the other agencies and he should certainly stay there. So the fellow, after 17 years in the plant, with two children is out on the street, without a job. I don't know whether the Corporations Auxiliary will take care of him or not.

"That man was not a typical spy. It was not his ambition to become a stool-pigeon, or spy, or, as we call them, a rat. He did not mean to be that at all, he was just hooked into it."

The Roy Williams tragedy is not unusual. It is typical. An ex-officer of the National Corporation Service admitted that of some 300 operatives upon whom he had kept records, over 200 were hooked men. The approach is nearly always the same for all the agencies. Mr. Gray, roving operative for Railway Audit, is on the stand:

SENATOR LA FOLLETTE. Now tell the committee, Mr. Gray, just how you approach these men. For instance, suppose there is a labor dispute going on and the Railway Audit & Inspection Co. is assigned to the job by a client. Now just how would you go about it? Suppose you found the type of man you thought was all right; just what kind of sales talk would you give him to get him to be your contact man?

MR. GRAY. Well, perhaps I would approach him as an insurance inspector.

SENATOR LA FOLLETTE. You never revealed your connection, did you, at the outset?

MR. GRAY. Oh, no.

SENATOR LA FOLLETTE. As connected with the Railway Audit & Inspection Co.?

MR. GRAY. No, sir; no sir.

Notice how positive Mr. Gray is that he never reveals his connection. There's a reason. It's a Railway Audit rule which is made very plain to all contact men. On May 24, 1935, Gray was reminded of that rule in a letter from his superior, L. D. Rice, vice-president. Rice is short and to the point. "As to hooked men . . . we never let them know who they are working for." But Gray is not at a loss — there are plenty of ways of representing himself. He need not always pose as an insurance inspector. He might be a newspaper man. Or,

SENATOR LA FOLLETTE. Have you ever suggested or inferred that you were representative of minority stockholders that were dissatisfied with the management?

MR. GRAY. Well, I might have; yes.

SENATOR LA FOLLETTE. That is one of the ways, is it not?

MR. GRAY. Yes; that is one of the ways. I might have done that.   . . .

SENATOR LA FOLLETTE. When the N.R.A. was still a law did you ever suggest to any of these men that you wanted to contact, that you were kind of checking up to find out how the N.R.A. was going, and leaving them with the impression that they might be engaged in a kind of patriotic effort on the part of the Government?

MR. GRAY. No, sir.

SENATOR LA FOLLETTE. You did not use that?

MR. GRAY. I cannot recall using that one; no, sir.

SENATOR LA FOLLETTE. I am surprised. You seem to be a very smart man.

MR. GRAY. I am just too smart to use that one, because that is involving the Government.

Maybe Gray of Railway Audit was telling the truth — maybe he was too smart to pose as a government official. But there is sworn testimony in the record that a Pinkerton operative did use exactly that line in trying to hook Charles Rigby, an Auto-Lite worker of Toledo, Ohio. Rigby would have been a good catch because he was a militant union man, chairman of his local. Perhaps the Pinkerton operative, in his anxiety to hook a man especially valuable at that time because of a strike situation, may be forgiven for not being as smart as Gray. The testimony of Rigby was particularly dramatic because the Pink who approached him was in the Senate chamber and heard every word of it. Rigby pointed him out as he testified.

SENATOR THOMAS. Mr. Rigby, has any attempt ever been made to hook you?
. . .

MR. RIGBY. Yes, sir; positively.

SENATOR THOMAS. When?

MR. RIGBY. A month and a half after Bart Furey came into the plant there was a man approached me at my house. He came into my home and he said he wanted to see me. He was a very well-educated man, dignified. He said he wanted to see me about something personal. My wife was sitting there and I said, "I am sorry but," I said, "I will not talk to you unless my wife is present." "Well," he said, "All right, it does not make much difference."

SENATOR THOMAS. Did the man give you his name?

MR. RIGBY. Yes.

SENATOR THOMAS. What was it?

MR. RIGBY. R. L. Bronson. He went on to state he was a representative of the N.R.A.

SENATOR THOMAS. He said he represented the N.R.A.?

MR. RIGBY. A representative of the N.R.A.; yes, sir.

SENATOR THOMAS. How could anyone represent the N.R.A.?

MR. RIGBY. I do not know. He was making investigations, an investigator of the N.R.A.

SENATOR THOMAS. A Government official?

MR. RIGBY. Yes, sir. . . .

SENATOR THOMAS. Did he mention that he was connected with the Government?

MR. RIGBY. Yes; that he was compiling statistics regarding chiseling and where they were paying low wages and they were working the workers long hours, above the code, and he said the Government wanted that, and he asked me if I could be of any service, if I would help him out. I said, "Certainly," I said, "I don't see any harm in that." I said, "Anything to help my fellow workers or help the Government," I said, "That is my duty." He said, "Well, the Government has appropriated so much money to compile these statistics." I said, "Well, as far as the money is concerned I would gladly work for nothing in order to get things straightened out, if I could be instrumental in doing that I would gladly do it for nothing." He said, "Well, the Government does not ask you to work for nothing." He said, "We will pay you $20 a week." He went on and he talked and talked.

SENATOR THOMAS. By "we" did he mean "we" or the Government will pay you $20 a week?

MR. RIGBY. The Government; the way he talked to me it was the Government. As I get it, they had to send the highest official. I never knew it until today, but they sent one of the highest officials of the Pinkerton Detective Agency to frame me and my family. . . .

SENATOR THOMAS. Did you ever see Bronson again?

MR. RIGBY. I saw him three times, three or four times, and

the last time he came to my house I told the business agent [of the union] . . . and he said, "Charlie," he said, "you have been framed." Well, after that I thought, "Well, I will see him again."

SENATOR THOMAS. Did you make any report to Bronson?

MR. RIGBY. Yes; I did.

SENATOR THOMAS. How many?

MR. RIGBY. I made reports for about 4 weeks.

SENATOR THOMAS. Where did you send them?

MR. RIGBY. I sent them to Book Cadillac Hotel, Detroit, Michigan.

SENATOR THOMAS. Addressed to whom?

MR. RIGBY. R. L. Bronson.

SENATOR THOMAS. What did you say in the reports?

MR. RIGBY. I just told him . . . where there was chiseling, and he said my reports are not satisfactory, that . . . was not what he wanted.

In the meantime, after this man told me I had been framed, he came to my house and I looked at him and I started in on him and I told him plenty. I said, "Mr. Bronson, if it is the last thing on earth I ever do I will get you, if you ever try to frame me and my family." He stood there, just looked, a big yellow rat, you know how they are, and he trembled, and he said, "Mr. Rigby, if you take that attitude," he said, "we'll forget the whole matter." I said, "Well, if you ever cross my path or cause my family any trouble," I said, "I will get you," and that man is present in this room today, and right there he is. (indicating).

Tense moment.

What would Bronson say? Would he admit the charge that he had posed as a government official? Not a chance. The agency crowd was admitting precious little — the truth had to be forced out of them. Nevertheless, Bronson did confess to a great deal, enough to substantiate Rigby's story:

SENATOR THOMAS. Mr. Bronson or Mr. Burnside — which is your proper name?

MR. BURNSIDE. Burnside, Senator.

. . .

SENATOR THOMAS. Will you state your occupation . . . ?

MR. BURNSIDE. I am assistant superintendent in the Detroit office of the Pinkerton Detective Agency.

. . .

SENATOR THOMAS. How many names have you used in your occupation for covering yourself, Mr. Burnside?

MR. BURNSIDE. Oh, I have used a great many names, Senator. I have been in the agency a great many years and necessarily our work requires using an alias a great many times.

SENATOR THOMAS. Name some of them.

MR. BURNSIDE. Well I have used the name of Bronson and I have used the name of Brunswick — oh, a number of them. I generally use a name with the same initials as mine, because it makes it easy to remember. It is customary in detective practice.

. . .

SENATOR THOMAS. Do you recognize Mr. Rigby?

MR. BURNSIDE. Yes.

SENATOR THOMAS. You heard his testimony?

MR. BURNSIDE. Yes, sir.

SENATOR THOMAS. Are the things which he has said true?

MR. BURNSIDE. No, sir.

. . .

SENATOR THOMAS. In what particular are they not true?

MR. BURNSIDE. Well, in a number of particulars. In the first place, the fact that he stated I was a Government officer is incorrect.

SENATOR THOMAS. What did you state you were?

MR. BURNSIDE. I told him that I represented certain people who were interested —

SENATOR THOMAS. (interrupting) What people?

MR. BURNSIDE. I did not tell him. I was not afraid to tell him that, because of the nature of the work, but I told him I represented certain people who were interested in getting this information that I spoke to him about.

SENATOR THOMAS. Did you represent certain people?

MR. BURNSIDE. I represented ourselves, yes; our agency.

SENATOR THOMAS. Did you imply that those certain people were people that were interested in the enforcement of the N.R.A. law?

MR. BURNSIDE. It has been a couple of years ago, Senator. As I recall it, I told him that we were interested in getting this information as to the violation of codes, chiseling, and any discrimination, violations in general of the practices laid down at that time.   . . .

SENATOR THOMAS. Did you ever use the name of the Pinkerton Detective Agency in his presence?

MR. BURNSIDE. No.

SENATOR THOMAS. You tried to sneak up on him, as it were, did you?

MR. BURNSIDE. Well, "sneak" is not a very pleasant word.

SENATOR THOMAS. Well, name your word for it.

MR. BURNSIDE. I wanted to make sure that Mr. Rigby had the necessary aptitude, and so on, for our work before I told him definitely who we were. He appeared to be the type of man that we could use.

SENATOR THOMAS. You assumed he was worth $20 a week anyway?

MR. BURNSIDE. Yes.

SENATOR THOMAS. Is that your judgment?

MR. BURNSIDE. As a preliminary arrangement; yes. He was a young man who appeared to be highly intelligent, as I presume you will all grant me, he was a chap that was loyal to his family all the way through and appeared to be 100 per cent dependable and the type of man that I could have used.

Burnside, Pinkerton operative, was trying to make a spy out of Rigby. It was not his practice to hook just any worker. Not at all. Rigby was to be given the honor of spying on his fellow workers because he was just the right type of man for the job—highly intelligent, loyal, dependable. No ordinary person would do. The Pinkertons made it a practice, before attempting to make a stool-pigeon out of an honest workman, to be sure that he was honest. At least that's their story. Mr. Rossetter, general manager, also testified that they were concerned about the character of their informants. "We make inquiries in the neighborhood in which they live to learn what their standing in the community is, whether they are considered honest, trustworthy, law-abiding people." Evidently only the best people were considered qualified for the job of selling out their fellow workers.

Perhaps it was a coincidence that these best people with good character were also important in their union. This, the Pinkertons argued, was of no especial significance, a mere happen-so. Maybe. Charles Rigby was a prominent union man. And so was Charles Forwerck, also of Toledo, and also one of Burnside's prospects. On the stand Burnside told a similar story about his unsuccessful attempt to hook Forwerck, worker in the Libbey-Owens Ford Glass Company, and on the executive board of the union. This time, according to Forwerck's affidavit, Burnside posed as the representative of some Detroit attorneys who in turn represented one of the largest motor corporations. Same palaver about not wanting any information that would hurt anybody in any way etc. etc.; same offer of money for the reports — this time, however, only $60 a month (compared to Rigby's $20 a week). It appears that Burnside underrated this new prospect. There is little doubt that Forwerck could have made a first class spy; as a matter of fact he did a tip-top job on Burnside himself! Here is Forwerck's account from the record:

He did not want to talk in front of my wife, and as a result I decided to find out what I could about him. After he left the house, I saw him walk over toward a car, several blocks away and I got into my car, turned the corner, and caught up with him as he was driving in his. I noted down the license number, an Ohio license, 9562-C. He was driving a 1934 Pontiac sedan, green-colored. He had previously told me that his name was Blackburn. I checked his license number with the Automobile Club in Toledo and discovered that the license had been issued to Ray L. Burnside, of 4591 Westway. I checked with the telephone book and found his number to be Lawndale 1565.

Now this, you will grant, was not a bad piece of work for an amateur sleuth. But just imagine . . . if only Forwerck had been possessed of that extra amount of character which the agency found a man needed to become a high-grade stool pigeon! Then, under the expert guidance of Burnside and the other famous Pinks, what a career would have been his — perhaps he would have become the greatest labor spy in American history! How unfortunate that this worker who had come through the preliminary Pinkerton investigation of his special qualifications of honesty, loyalty and trustworthiness, with flying colors, should at the crucial moment fail them — all because of some silly notion in his mind that it was a dirty trick to spy on his fellow workers.

Don't make the mistake of supposing that the Pinkertons lied when they said they made inquiries into the character of the men they were about to hook. They definitely do make an intensive investigation, as Mr. George A. Patterson, a steel worker at the Carnegie-Illinois Steel Company in Chicago found out to his amazement. Perhaps it was again just a coincidence that besides being a man of good character, Mr. Patterson was also a strong union man who was both an employees' representative in the company union and president of the Independent Steel Organization which rose up in rebellion against the company union. Mr. Patterson's story is the familiar one: invalid sister, indicating need of money; key man in the union; harmless sales talk about reports that would harm nobody. The only new feature is the surprising degree to which Mr. Patterson had been investigated. Mr. Patterson on the witness stand:

On Lincoln's Birthday I returned from work and I found a heavy burly man in my home. I was quite upset about it. I wanted to know how this man got in my home. It so happened that I have an invalid sister who is at home at all times, and she happened to allow this man in. I felt rather mad to find this stranger in my house. So I asked him what his business was. He said he had a proposition to make to me. I could not understand what he had to do with me. So he took me aside into my little kitchenette in the apartment and started a very fluent salesmanship talk. He said that he represented the Fidelity Bond Company of the Empire State Building, New York, and he went on to state how interested they were in trying to increase the profits of the stockholders, and that he believed that there was trouble between employees and managers, and that he thought I could help.

I did not say very much but I listened to his story. He was very forceful, and after a while I asked him what I could do to help him in any way, he stated that I was a man of very good character, how they had investigated me and knew I had worked for almost 12 years with the Illinois Steel Company — the Carnegie-Illinois Steel; it is merged now — and he knew I had been in the roll-shop department; he could tell all about me . . . He could tell me I was a good church member, that I was general superintendent of the Sunday school where I attended, and so on. The man evidently had investigated my character . . . In fact, he knew almost as much about myself as I did. When he got through he said, "How would you like to do this for us? We will not ask you to do anything for us that will get you into trouble. Just go about your business in the usual way and make reports." By this time I thought this was a very peculiar situation, and I felt kind of peculiar. He sort of repulsed me, because I had never been approached in any way by anybody like him before.

Mr. Patterson was evidently a newcomer to the trade union movement. Probably this was the first time he had held office in a union. To older, more experienced labor leaders, hooking is not new. They have known of it for many years and many of them have met with it, personally. They know how to handle it. They report immediately to the union.

Mr. Carl Holderman, the district manager for the American Full-Fashioned Hosiery Workers, had been "contacted" several times so he knew what to expect when, in 1929, he was visited by a Mr. Ralph Robinson "representing the American Bankers Association." Mr. Holderman was a top ranking officer, not in a local union, but in the national organization. Don't be surprised, then, to learn that as vice president of the national organization he was worth more than the ordinary hooked man. "He offered $150 a month [more than the others were offered, but not a patch on the rake-off of James C. Cronin, one-time President of the Central Labor Union of Philadelphia, who was paid $200 a week for his services as Operative 03] if I would be willing to supply them with information as to possible strike situations that might occur in the near future . . . I immediately got in touch with the officers of our union, and we decided to see what else he had to offer."

Mr. Phil E. Ziegler, the secretary-treasurer of the Brotherhood of Railway Clerks, was another labor leader who was on to the hooking activities of the spy agencies. When the night watchman of the building owned by the Railways Clerks informed him that he had been approached by a Mr. Bradley, Mr. Ziegler knew what to do. He had Jones play along with Bradley (real name, Samuel H. Brady, Pinkerton superintendent of the Cincinnati office) until they got the goods on him. Bradley-Brady pulled the familiar line with a new slant, "On our Executive Board we have fifty men (50), we have certain state Senators, Congressmen and many prominent men such as Charles Evans Hughes, Henry Ford, John D. Rockefeller, Dr. Parkes S. Cadman, Father Ryan, Dr. Finney, the great surgeon . . ." The union officials were not convinced.

Don't get the impression from these unsuccessful attempts at hooking, that the agencies always fail. They often succeed. Too often. Sometimes, as you can imagine, their success means the ruination of the hooked man's life. Often the men of character that they so carefully choose, to trick into becoming spies, go steadily to pieces until there is little character left in them. Occasionally a hooked man is able to break away from the agency, make peace with his conscience, and start life all over again. More often they remain trapped. One of the most pitiful instances of the terrible harm done by hooking is the case of the young man who never could get over the feeling of horror within himself that he had betrayed his fellow workers. Even after making a clean breast of his spying activities, even after being absolved of all blame by the union heads, he was so overcome with remorse and shame that if by chance he would pass a vegetable store window in which the sign "Northern Spy" apples was displayed, he would break out into a cold sweat and his heart would pound like a trip-hammer.

Hooking is the method most commonly employed when the agency finds it necessary to use as its informant one of the workers already in the factory. But sometimes the plant setup is such that an outside operative can be brought in without causing undue suspicion. The agencies usually recruit these outside operatives by the "blind ad" method:

SENATOR LA FOLLETTE. How do you get operatives when you need new ones?

MR. ROSS. Why we are constantly recruiting them, under ordinary circumstances, by advertising and through blind ads, and then we interview them and we select them through the process of elimination. We have them write reports, giving them subjects to write on, give them a talk and just let them come back and see how much of it they get. A mental test, I should say it was.

Unemployed workers hunting for jobs turn to the Help Wanted section of the newspapers. You know what they find there:

HELP WANTED

MACHINIST: General all-round machinist; preferably experienced with big tools and heavy work; hourly rate and bonus. Give shop experience, age and phone. Box 524. Press.

PLANER HANDS: Heavy work, expansion program; highest hourly rate to producers; give details of experience, references and phone. Box 13772. Plain Dealer.

RUBBER WORKERS: On sundries and specialties; can make up to 80¢ per hour, depending on production. Explain class of work, machines experienced on, age and phone number. Box 7372. Plain Dealer.

STRANDERS: And roughers for merchant mill on round, hex and square stock; hourly rate plus tonnage. In reply give description, full history and phone. Address Box 6418. Press.

These are real ads taken from The *Cleveland Press* and *Cleveland Plain Dealer*. They look like any other ads. But they are not. For the unemployed worker who hopefully writes to any one of these Box Numbers, they may be dynamite. These four harmless looking offers of jobs were "blind ads" inserted by the Corporations Auxiliary Co. They were the bait to lure workers hungry for jobs into the agency trap.

Any applicant who writes an intelligent reply to a blind ad is notified to call for an interview at a stated address. The name on the door of the office may be John Smith Company or Green Engineering Corporation or any name — except the name of the detective agency. The job-seeker is then given a "mental test," i.e., he may be asked to write a detailed report then and there of what he did that day, including all the people he talked to and what they said; or he may be given an ordinary literacy test, etc. If the interviewer is satisfied that he is capable, he is told that a job will be found for him at such and such a factory; he will receive his wages for his work at the factory, and an additional sum for the daily reports he is to write. The applicant next applies at the factory, is given the job at once, and his career as stool-pigeon is begun.

The whole procedure from beginning to end, from blind ad to union-smashing is beautifully illustrated in two affidavits from the record. The first is the story of John Mohacsi, a machinist who answered a blind ad and was molded into a spy; the second is a union official's account of Mohacsi's activities as a spy.

John Mohacsi, being duly sworn deposes and says:

That I reside at 30–26 49th Street, Astoria, Long Island, New York. That the following statements are made of my own free will and accord.

I have been working as a machinist since 1919. I started as an apprentice in the Trenton shop of the Pennsylvania Railroad and have, since that time, worked in many of the companies throughout the metropolitan area as an experienced machinist and tool and die maker.

In and about May 1935, while I was employed by the Atlantic Base and Iron Works of Brooklyn, New York, I answered an advertisement in the New York American, a paper published daily in the city of New York, calling for an experienced machinist. I received a letter on the letterhead of the Atlantic Production Company, 1775 Broadway, New York City, to come in for an interview. I was interviewed by a Mr. J. C. Carter, of that office who stated that his was a firm of consulting engineers and that if they placed me on a job I would have to report as to the conditions existing in the plant. I was also given a literacy test.

I heard no more from this Atlantic Production Company until November 1935, when I again received a letter from Carter on the letterhead of that company. I was then employed by the Fairchild Aerial Camera Corporation of Woodside, Long Island, N. Y. I was then again interviewed by J. C. Carter and told that they had a job for me. The job was with the Worthington Pump Company at Harrison, New Jersey.

I was to be employed as a tool maker at 78¢ per hour. In addition to this I was to get $50.00 per month for my reports to the Atlantic Production Company from Carter.

I was given instructions by Carter that I was to make reports every day concerning the type of men I was working with; whether any of the men were constantly complaining about conditions; to get to know what my fellow workers were thinking about and their attitude toward their pay and working conditions. I was also told that when I incorporated any of the complaints of the men, I was to make sure to state the names of the men. I was told to report what "I see" and what "I hear". I was told, in January 1936, by L. H. (Pat Stewart) to join the union and to make myself a leader among the men so as to influence their attitude toward their employer. I was also asked to report what fraternal lodge or union most of the men belonged to; how it affects their work and my specific instructions stated that if I thought my acquaintance might be widened by joining the lodge or union, to contact that Atlantic Production Company about the matter. I. was also instructed that if I was able to be elected from my department as a delegate to the lodge, I should do so in order that I may become a real leader among the men.

I was given a letter to Mr. Bennett, general manager of the Worthington Pump Company and was in turn turned over to the employment manager. After three weeks of making reports, I was turned over to Pat Stewart. Up until January 20, 1937, when I made my last report, my contact was with Pat Stewart.

On or about January 4th, 1936, Pat Stewart sent me a letter to come in to see him. In the ordinary course of my work, I would make personal visits bi-monthly to the office to report. When I came to the office, I noticed that the name Atlantic Production Company was no longer on the door, and there appeared the name International Auxiliary Corporation. At this time, Pat Stewart told me that he wanted me to join the union which was organizing at the plant. He handed me the application card of the Tool, Die, and Metal Workers' Union of which Mr. Rubicz was the organizer. This union later became a local of the I.A.M. affiliated with the A. F. of L., local #1560. He told me that I was to join up with the union and to make detailed reports of what went on at the meetings.

Thereafter I wrote out an application for membership to the union and became a member of same. Twice a month I would send in detailed reports on the meetings of the union . . . In accordance with my instructions from Pat Stewart, I reported on any radicals found in the plant or in the union. In accordance with these instructions, I did report the names and identities of any such radicals . . .

John Mohacsi.

That Mohacsi carried out his instructions to report on "radicals" is proven by the following affidavit. It proves also that he had been taught the customary agency definition of a radical — a man who belongs to a union.

Steve Rubicz, being duly sworn deposes and says:

That I am business representative of Unity Lodge #1560 of the International Association of Machinists affiliated with the A. F. of L., 315 Plane Street, Newark, New Jersey. That I was business agent of the Machinists, Tool and Foundry Workers local 401 which later became the present Unity Lodge #1560 of the International Association of Machinists.

John Mohacsi, in January 1936, wrote in an application for membership in what was then the Machinists, Tool and Foundry Workers local 401. He stated that he was employed in the Worthington Pump Company. At that time we had about 18 members in the tool room of the Worthington Pump Company. A few weeks after Mohacsi became a member, these men came to see me and told me that they were dropping their union membership. They stated that they had been informed by the company that it knew that they were members of the union and that they know all about the activities of the union. They were warned by the company that they had better drop their membership if they wanted to retain their positions. I am not stating the names of the men because of the fact that they are still employed by the company and it might jeopardize their positions if their names were stated. Practically all of the 18 resigned from the union. It was common knowledge among the employees of the Worthington Pump Company that the company was in a position of knowing whether or not they did join the union.

In or about May 1936 this local amalgamated with the International Association of Machinists and became local #1560. In and about September 1936, two members of our local secured positions at the Worthington Pump Company. Within two weeks they were both discharged without any reason having been given. Their names of course were known to Mohacsi and he, no doubt, reported this to the company.

Many of the employees of the Worthington Pump Company who have been with the company many years, have expressed a desire to join the union. But they have stated to me that they could not join because of the spy system of the company which would jeopardize their positions. For this reason the union has been unable to organize or secure any members in the said company. Mohacsi has been exposed as a spy in the employ of the International Auxiliary Corporation.

STEVE RUBICZ

Unemployed workers scan the Help Wanted section of the newspapers and apply for jobs for which they are qualified. They need the jobs. They are out of work and must have money. The jobs are offered them — with the seemingly harmless string attached, that they must write secret reports. Before long they are lured into the agency trap. They have become stool-pigeons.

Factory workers whose wages are not enough to meet their needs are offered extra money for writing seemingly innocent reports.

Before long they are lured into the agency trap. They are hooked. They have become stool-pigeons.

In this manner thousands of innocent men have been ensnared into becoming spies. In similar fashion, thousands of innocent girls have been trapped into becoming prostitutes. Is there any material difference between the agency operative hooking an innocent worker, and the pimp hooking an innocent girl? Even the money returns to the principals are comparable — the incomes of the heads of the large spy agency chains would not be sneered at by any head of a chain of brothels. The two "industries" are alike in technique, profits, morals and ethics.

V. The Rats' Code

JOHN ANDREWS was paid $40 a month for spying on his pal Dick Frankensteen. That's $480 a year. Rigby was offered $20 a week. That's $1040 a year. Roszel, Mohacsi, Shults and the others probably fall somewhere in between. Now $480 to $1000 is not a great deal of money. But the spying business is like every other business in capitalist society — low wages to the men who do the actual work, and huge returns to the directors and owners. While Andrews was receiving $480 for his year's work, one of his bosses, Dan Ross, the general manager, was receiving over 100 times as much — $50,000. And that wasn't all — for Ross. The pattern among our big industrialists is to throw in a reward — to themselves — for the fine work their employees have done. Corporations Auxiliary was no exception. Besides his $50,000 a year salary, Ross was given a bonus of 10% of the gross receipts. Not a bad arrangement for Mr. Ross as you can see from a glance at the gross annual income of Corporations Auxiliary:

1933	$284,847.78
1934	$489,131.11
1935	$518,215.26

Take 10% of each of those figures and add it to $50,000 and you have Mr. Ross's annual income. Notice that this bonus scheme stimulated Mr. Ross to get more work out of his employees every year, so that by 1935 he had really made good: his total salary for that year was higher than that of the President of the United States!

Nor did the general manager get all the pickings. There was still enough money left in the Corporations Auxiliary safe to take care of the other big shots in the firm. Mr. James H. Smith, "harmonizing-conditions" Smith, the president of Corporations Auxiliary and its subsidiaries, was not left out in the cold. According to his testimony he was supposed to get $15,000 a year from each of five operating companies. That would give him $75,000 aɩ nually, but for some reason which he didn't explain, he drew down only $48,000 in 1935. But before you begin to worry about whether Smith could live on that paltry sum, remember that was just his salary — his bonus and dividends are not counted in.

Mr. Weber, the secretary and treasurer of the outfit, must have enjoyed himself as he counted the money due him in 1935 — $30,-000. That came to a little less than $600 a week. It wasn't even a third of what he had to count out for Ross; nevertheless it was enough to scrape along on, and since the business was growing Mr. Weber could hope for a raise.

The Pinkertons did a bigger business. Their gross annual income for 1933 to 1935 was as follows:

1933	$1,466,530.54
1934	$2,187,240.52
1935	$2,318,039.18

Their income from their industrial service alone was almost twice as much as the gross annual income of Corporations Auxiliary. In 1934 it was approximately $900,000; in 1935, approximately $1,-000,000; and for the first 7 months of 1936 it was approximately $550,000.

But in spite of their huge volume of business, Pinkerton's salary situation was something frightful. Mr. Rossetter, who told a touching story of how he had worked himself down from office boy to chief clerk, to operative, to assistant superintendent, and finally to general manager, was grossly underpaid. In 1935 his salary was a measly $10,000 and his bonus a mere $2,000. Only $12,000 a year! Compare the salaries of Pinkerton's Rossetter to Corporations' Ross and the injustice becomes apparent at once. It's almost as though Rossetter were still an office boy.

And the worst of it was that Rossetter couldn't complain. It would have been different if Mr. Robert A. Pinkerton, the president of the agency, were drawing a huge salary. But he wasn't. Mr. Rossetter knew that what little work President Pinkerton did, he did for nothing. Mr. Pinkerton received no salary at all. It was true, of course, that the agency, in 1935, declared a dividend of $185,000. It was true, too, that Mr. Pinkerton's slice of that dividend melon was $129,500. But since Mr. Pinkerton owned 70% of the stock in the agency, the $129,500 was justly due him. Rossetter was experienced enough in business to know that it is customary and proper for the lion's share to go to the men who own, not to the men who work.

Now if you have been squirming as you read about these salaries because your own annual income looks tiny by comparison, remember that America is still the land of opportunity. You too, have a chance to crash into the Big Money. The way is clear — but it means hard work. Are you willing to apply yourself? Are you willing to spend fifteen minutes a day in earnest study? If you are, then the Road to Success lies before you. An unusual career is open to ambitious young men and women — the Chance of a Lifetime — the opportunity to become a Stool-Pigeon. The National Manufacturers Syndicate, an affiliate of the Sherman Service, tells you how. All you need do is enroll for their correspondence course, then study, study, study. Here are a few sample instructions from their 24-page booklet entitled "Correspondence Course of Training for an Industrial Operative":

First Instruction Sheet

There is nothing about your relationship with your fellow workers which can be considered underhand or deceitful . . . Our work is most honorable, humanitarian, and very important, and must be recognized as such.

Second Instruction Sheet

It is very plain that in order for us to be successful we must conduct our work in an invisible manner. The ordinary worker, in his ignorance, is apt to misunderstand our motives if he knows of our presence and identity in the plant. You will really be engaged in human engineering — but in order that you may succeed, no one is to know of your association with us or the character of work which you are doing.

THIRD INSTRUCTION SHEET

The rules and regulations of our organization exclude even one's close friends and families from any knowledge as to the details of any assignments a representative may receive . . .

It will be your duty to make up and mail in a detailed report for each day as to when you begin work, when you quit, what you did, what you saw, and what you heard in connection with the particular assignment in which you were engaged . . .

You will receive frequent instructions from us which you are to mail back to us together with envelope in which it was sent as soon as you have read them carefully . . .

Live strictly in accordance with your apparent earnings in the plant. Do not spend money freely. Such action would attract attention at once and would ruin your chance of making your work successful.

When assigned to inside work in mill or factory, get a rooming place the same as any other worker would do. Do not share it with others. The presence of an outsider would interfere with the writing of your confidential reports and making up of expense accounts.

Should it ever become necessary for you to explain to the police your presence in any town, never under any circumstances admit to a police officer your connection with this organization. If the story you tell them does not satisfy them, ask to see the police chief and to him only communicate your identity by name and number and request him to get in touch with us. When he communicates with us you will be dismissed at once.

In writing your reports see that you are not observed by fellow workers, the landlady, or others. When leaving the room

Senate Probers Examine Striker "Persuader"

(Underwood and Underwood)

"Six little Pinks sitting in a row": 1. Shoemack; 2. Dudley;
3. Pinkerton; 4. Rossetter; 5. Pugmire; 6. Clark   (*Acme*)

Raymond J. Burns and W. Sherman Burns, heads of the Burns
agency   (*Pictures, Inc.*)

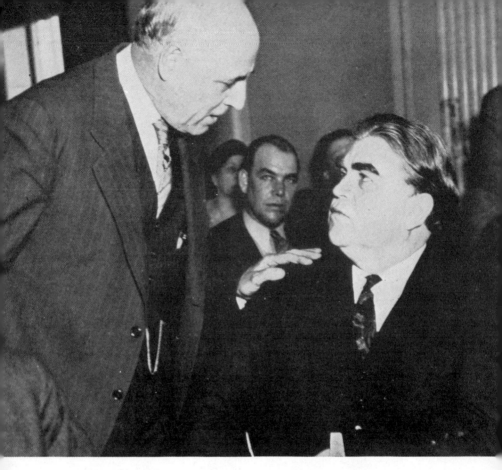

John L. Lewis, interested observer at the hearings   (*Acme*)

be sure that you leave no memoranda lying around. Tear them up into minute parts before throwing into waste basket, or better still, use the toilet hopper or burn . . .

FOURTH INSTRUCTION SHEET

Both your representative number and your case series number must appear on every report and expense slip. Never use your name, or this organization, or the client's name. When necessary refer to us as "The Service" and to the client as "The Client" . . .

In mixing with your fellow-workers never allow yourself to become intoxicated and never under any circumstances permit yourself to mix up with women. Do not spend excessively. Make no display of a roll of bills and be sure when you send in your expense account that you make mention of money spent for treats of fellow-workers . . .

In giving conversations always give the name of the man or his number, then tell what you said to him and what he says to you. In all these conversations try to talk about the work so as to find out how each man feels about the foreman and superintendent or anyone else in authority. You want to find out when the union meets, if there is a union. Then maybe we will have you arrange to attend their meetings so that we can see just what is going on, and be able to report whether any of the men where you are at work are members of the union. Be sure to report whether any agitation is going on in town anywhere.

Remember we are unalterably opposed to all cliques, radicalists, and disturbing elements who try to create discontentment, suspicion, and unfriendliness on the part of the workers toward the employer. The minds of those who are dissatisfied and disgruntled must be changed. As our representative, you must find out first of all who are the dissatisfied ones; then cultivate their friendship and win their confidence. You will then be in a position to help us eliminate discontentment.

Be forewarned before you enroll for this course that more than diligent habits of study are required to win success in the spy business. You must be daring. You must be prepared to throw overboard your moral scruples. You must be hard. You must learn to lie easily and often. You must convince yourself that practices which most people regard as definitely wrong, are definitely right. You must be slippery, shrewd, sharp, sneaky. You must not hesitate to beat the law where you can and break the law where you must. Success came to Corporations Auxiliary, the Pinkerton Agency, the Burns Agency, the Sherman Service, Railway Audit & Inspection and the other top-notchers, only because they had learned these things.

Let us look at the record.

In 1933, the Chrysler Corporation owed to Corporations Auxiliary $61,627.48. The agency submitted its bill and received payment.

In 1934, the Chrysler Corporation owed to Corporations Auxiliary $76,411.81. The agency submitted its bill and received payment.

In 1935, the Chrysler Corporation owed to Corporations Auxiliary $72,611.89. But now a curious thing happened. The agency did *not* submit its bill and receive payment. Instead, *it submitted four bills.*

Only the first, for $19,946.55, was from Corporations Auxiliary.

The second, for $19,447.09, was from Smith & Weber.

The third, for $16,910.58, was from the Equitable Auditing & Publishing Co.

And the fourth, for $16,307.67, was from the International Auxiliary Co.

The total is $72,611.89, which is what the Chrysler Corporation owed to Corporations Auxiliary for 1935. Then why all the monkey business? Why did the agency in 1935 have to pull out of a hat a Smith and Weber letterhead, and an Equitable Auditing letterhead? What trick was being performed in 1935 that wasn't staged in '33 or '34?

Watch carefully.

SENATOR LA FOLLETTE. Mr. Smith, are you familiar with the Securities Act . . .?

MR. SMITH. I do not think so, Senator.

SENATOR LA FOLLETTE. Are you familiar with the regulations under that act requiring a corporation to report to the Securities and Exchange Commission all payments for services in excess of $20,000 made by it to any firm, person, or corporation?

MR. SMITH. It seems to me I have read something of that sort.

SENATOR LA FOLLETTE. Well, now, have you any reason which you can give to the committee as to why these bills were split up in 1935 and not split up in 1934?

MR. SMITH. None that I can give you, sir; no, sir.

SENATOR LA FOLLETTE. Do you think that the Securities and Exchange Act had anything to do with it?

MR. SMITH. I might imagine some such thing, but I have no knowledge of it.

Now we begin to understand. Smith hasn't been very helpful (he gets a tremendous salary for knowing almost nothing, doesn't he?), but Senator La Follette's suspicions give us a clue. The Chrysler Corporation wanted to evade the law that required it to report to the S.E.C. all payments it made above $20,000; the Chrysler Corporation was too embarrassed or afraid to make known the fact that it had paid $72,611.89 to a spy agency. It asked Corporations Auxiliary to help it beat the law, and the *agency obliged by splitting its bill into 4 parts no one of which was above $20,000.* Under this arrangement Chrysler could pay what it owed without reporting it — thus beating the law.

Shady business, of course. We might be prepared to believe that the dick agency would be partner to such a deal, but what about the Chrysler Corporation? Would that great firm stoop so low? Perhaps it's all a mistake, perhaps our suspicions are wrong.

Alas, no. The mighty Chrysler Corporation and Corporations Auxiliary did conspire together to beat the law. It was, in fact,

Chrysler's idea — and the agency did not hesitate to do its crooked part. When Dan Ross was asked why Corporations Auxiliary's method of billing was changed in 1935, he gave the whole show away:

> MR. ROSS. That was changed at the request of one of the officers — I do not know whom — on account of the Securities Act.
>
> SENATOR LA FOLLETTE. It was changed at the request of one of the officers of the Chrysler Corporation?
>
> MR. ROSS. Yes, sir.   . . .
>
> SENATOR LA FOLLETTE. It originated with them, you are positive?
>
> MR. ROSS. Oh, absolutely.
>
> SENATOR LA FOLLETTE. Now, obviously, as far as the Corporations Auxiliary Co. was concerned, you were willing to cooperate, after you had received this request from the Chrysler Corporation, in breaking down your bills for identical service, so they would not have to report?
>
> MR. ROSS. I so informed Mr. Weber, and . . . the sending of those bills was in accordance with that procedure.
>
> SENATOR LA FOLLETTE. So as to enable the Chrysler Corporation, according to your testimony, to avoid the necessity of reporting, as required by law?
>
> MR. ROSS. I suppose so.

What Corporations Auxiliary could do for Chrysler, the Pinkertons could do for General Motors. Were General Motors officials worried lest detailed Pinkerton bills passing through the accounting department might reveal the fact that spies were in the plant? Then the Pinks could relieve them of their fears. Two bills could be submitted: one, long and detailed with all the dope in it — for the corporation officials, who would destroy it after reading; the other, short and meaningless, with no tell-tale information on it — for the accountants and the files. What troublesome information, for example, could the accountants glean from the following harmless-looking bill?

G. O. 9 19332
April 30, 1935

General Motors Corporation, Dr.
    In Account with J. S. Smith, 154 Nassau Street, New York,
    N. Y. :

For Professional Services......................	$2,780.68
Travelling Expenses.......................	865.54
Telephone and Telegraph...................	946.42
Publications..............................	157.02
	$4,749.66

Approved for Payment. Return to Audit Dept. For Final
    Audit.
Approved for Final Audit — R. A. M.
PAID OCT. 4, 1935; Ck. No. C 30298
265 — R O.K. J. Eaton 27a
OK NMP OK H. W. A.

Could you tell from this bill that the $4,749.66 went in reality to the Pinkerton Agency for its industrial service? Not evident in any way, is it? But wasn't it just as meaningless to General Motors officials as it might be to the accountants? (Or to snooping government officials?) Oh, no. They understood it because, you remember, this bill was accompanied by a detailed one which explained Mr. Smith's "professional services," etc.

Do you find it utterly fantastic that General Motors, one of the greatest corporations in the world, should have asked the Pinks to bill them in this sneaking fashion? And that the Pinkerton Agency (established 1850), which prides itself that it is superior to other agencies, should have complied with General Motors' request? Then look at the sworn testimony:

MR. HALE. [former labor-relations director] . . . I worked it out with Mr. McMullen that we didn't think it desirable to have a lot of this detailed information going through our accounting department files.

SENATOR LA FOLLETTE. Why?

MR. HALE. For the reason it was the type of information we just didn't think was good business to have scattered around through the department.

SENATOR LA FOLLETTE. Why?

MR. HALE. Well—(Laughter).

SENATOR LA FOLLETTE. As a matter of fact, Mr. Hale, you did not want it to get back to the employees that you were getting this kind of information, if you will pardon me for asking a leading question to save time.

MR. HALE. I don't know that that was entirely the reason, sir. A good many things are not understood, Senator, by people who do not understand the whole picture.

SENATOR LA FOLLETTE. I will grant you that. But, for example, Mr. Hale, it is not an accounting practice of this efficient corporation, is it, to digest or think up strange headings for bills for equipment, and parts and materials, is it? The Steel Corporation does not bill you for wooden ware, does it? (Laughter)

MR. HALE. No, sir.   . . .

SENATOR LA FOLLETTE. . . . You put into effect, or had an arrangement with Pinkerton's whereby those detailed bills, which you thought inadvisable to have going through the accounting department, came through in the form of a breakdown into four or five different heads?

MR. HALE. Yes, sir.

SENATOR LA FOLLETTE. And then later on you began to get bills from clerks in Pinkerton's, like J. S. Smith, for professional services during 1 month, $2,850. Now, I am asking you if those were typical of the bills you received? . . .

MR. HALE. We received two bills. We received a detailed bill . . . and a summary bill for purposes of going through our accounting department. On the basis of the detailed bill it gave me a chance to audit the over-all bill.

SENATOR LA FOLLETTE. What did you do with the detailed bill?

MR. HALE. Destroyed it, sir.

SENATOR LA FOLLETTE. The bills that were left in the records of the General Motors' offices were really not reflectory of the kind of service you were obtaining, were they?

MR. HALE. I would say they were; yes, sir; very definitely.

SENATOR LA FOLLETTE. Would you say a bill, from J. S. Smith, who Mr. Rossetter testified was a clerk in his office, for professional services, amounting to, if my recollection serves me correctly, in 1 month to $2,850, and traveling and telephone expenses around $900, revealed the type of service that Pinkerton was rendering to your organization?

MR. HALE. Those bills were subsequent to my time, and I will ask Mr. Anderson to answer that question.

SENATOR LA FOLLETTE. What would you say, Mr. Anderson?

• • •

MR. ANDERSON. No, sir.

Of course it's unfair to put more than a little of the blame on the agencies. In both these cases the shady idea came originally from the clients, Chrysler and General Motors. All that the agencies did was to fall in with the scheme without any quibbling. They obeyed their master's voice. The companies that paid the bills were calling the tune.

They called a good many tunes — some of them definitely off key to anybody not made tone-deaf by contact with dick agencies. For example, both Chrysler and General Motors ordered their spy service extended to *plants other than their own!* Chrysler bought supplies and equipment from firms not subsidiary to the Chrysler Corporation. Mr. Allen P. Hascall, who was in charge of the purchase of materials, testified that he felt it was his job to keep a steady flow of materials coming into the plant, so he asked Corporations Auxiliary to make "surveys" of the vendor plants. Corporations Auxiliary obliged. It made surveys, too, of plants not yet selling to Chrysler. It even made surveys of vendors to competitors of Chrysler! And in no case were the officials of these plants advised that Chrysler was spying on them through Corporations Auxiliary. Pretty business!

SENATOR LA FOLLETTE. Is it your policy to ask for reports on all vendors who supply an appreciable amount of materials necessary for the complete operation of the Chrysler plants?
MR. HASCALL. Yes, sir.   .   .   .

SENATOR LA FOLLETTE. Is it your practice to secure such a report before you purchase any material from a new source of supply?
MR. HASCALL. I frequently do that.
.   .   .

SENATOR LA FOLLETTE. When you have a vendors' survey made . . . do you advise any of the officers of that company that you are having such a survey made?
MR. HASCALL. No sir.   .   .   .

SENATOR LA FOLLETTE. Is it not often true that your competitors use some of these vendors?
MR. HASCALL. I would say so.

Does Chrysler's practice of injecting their paid spies into the other fellow's plants seem just a trifle — er — unusual? Well, it didn't seem so to General Motors — their only complaint was that their own spies, the Pinks, didn't get them enough information on their vendors' business:

SENATOR LA FOLLETTE. Now, Mr. Hale; were you interested in information concerning labor conditions and organizational activities in the equipment and suppliers of General Motors?
MR. HALE. I was interested if there was threatened trouble.
SENATOR LA FOLLETTE. Did Pinkertons furnish you such information?

MR. HALE. Not as completely as I wished they had.
SENATOR LA FOLLETTE. They did furnish you some?
MR. HALE. Yes, sir.

If you think all this spying in their own plants and in the plants of their vendors is becoming a hopeless tangle, here's a word of warning — "You ain't seen nothin' yet." General Motors put the Pinkertons on still another tack — they had to spy on the Corporations Auxiliary! *The spies for General Motors were asked to spy on the spies for Chrysler.*

Senator La Follette hands a Pinkerton ledger sheet to Edward S. Clark, manager of the Pinkerton Cleveland office:

SENATOR LA FOLLETTE. Mr. Clark, do you know what C.A.C. stands for? There are 11 entries for C.A.C. What is that?
MR. CLARK. I think that is the Corporations Auxiliary Co.
SENATOR LA FOLLETTE. What were you doing on that job?
MR. CLARK. Well, we were trying to find out whether or not information they were securing was being passed to a competitor.   .   .   .

SENATOR LA FOLLETTE. Now, why did you concentrate on Corporations Auxiliary?
MR. CLARK. Well, it was my understanding that those folks were doing a good deal of work for this particular competitor.
SENATOR LA FOLLETTE. Which one?
MR. CLARK. Chrysler . . .

How the spy system grows! What sorry practices our business leaders feel themselves forced to indulge in, because of the pressure of competitive capitalist industry.

But we've not reached the end even yet. Not only do the agencies spy on workers and vendors, and on the operatives of other agencies, but they even spy on their own spies! They can't even trust themselves. Robert W. Coates, a Burns operative, admitted this. He was being questioned about a report he had written about a union meeting of bakery workers which he had attended. (See Appendix C.)

SENATOR LA FOLLETTE. As a matter of fact did you not take part in this meeting and make these suggestions for the purpose of establishing confidence in the minds of the other people there concerning yourself and your *bona fide* connection as a worker for a bakery?

MR. COATES. Well, it is certain I didn't go in there and tell them I was a Burns detective. It is quite obvious from my reports on it.

SENATOR LA FOLLETTE. You even went so far as to express your fear there might be some stool-pigeons present.

MR. COATES. Why, I was satisfied there was.

SENATOR LA FOLLETTE. How could you tell? (Laughter)

MR. COATES. Senator, in my experience for the past twenty some years I have found out there is stools in every union organization.

SENATOR LA FOLLETTE. You did not think there were any other Burns stools there, did you?

MR. COATES. I didn't know. There might have been somebody there checking on me for all I knew. (Laughter)

· · ·

SENATOR THOMAS. Is that a common practice?

MR. COATES. For what?

SENATOR THOMAS. For Burns men to check on Burns men.

MR. COATES. Well, I have known them to.

The Burns agency had the "checking" habit. For a consideration, they would check anything and everybody. No, that's not quite true — Mr. W. Sherman Burns, secretary-treasurer of the William J. Burns International Detective Agency, testified that they "never shadowed any grand juries at any time." Trial juries — well, they were different, but grand juries, never.

SENATOR LA FOLLETTE. Do you recall the activities of your agency in connection with the prosecution of Harry Sinclair for refusing to answer questions before a Senate committee, engaged in investigating the Teapot Dome Oil scandals?

MR. W. SHERMAN BURNS. Yes, sir.

SENATOR LA FOLLETTE. Did not operatives of your agency shadow members of a Federal grand jury which indicted Sinclair?

MR. W. SHERMAN BURNS. Not in that case, or in no case. We never shadowed any grand juries at any time.

SENATOR LA FOLLETTE. Did you shadow the trial jurors in that case?

MR. W. SHERMAN BURNS. In the Sinclair case; yes.

SENATOR LA FOLLETTE. Pardon me for getting the question first about the grand jury. Is there any difference between shadowing grand jury members and trial jury members in your judgment?

MR. W. SHERMAN BURNS. I think so.

SENATOR LA FOLLETTE. In the field of morals or ethics?

MR. W. SHERMAN BURNS. Yes; I think so.

SENATOR LA FOLLETTE. Do you recall what the Supreme Court of the United States had to say about private detectives apropos of your activities in the Sinclair case?

. . .

MR. W. SHERMAN BURNS. No; I don't recall.

SENATOR LA FOLLETTE. Just to refresh your recollection I will read in part from the decision of the Supreme Court:

"The most exemplary resent having their footsteps dogged by private detectives. All know that men who accept such employment commonly lack fine scruples, and only wilfully misrepresent innocent conduct and manufacture charges."

Does that refresh your recollection?

MR. W. SHERMAN BURNS. Yes, sir.

It might be argued that the Supreme Court was a little too hard on the dicks when it said they "commonly lack fine scruples." Actually the scruples of the Burns outfit were so very, very fine that they could detect a difference in ethics between shadowing a grand jury and a trial jury.

One wonders what the Supreme Court would think of the latest wrinkle in shadowing. In Toledo, in 1935, there was a strike at the Chevrolet plant. Mr. Edward McGrady, the Assistant Secretary of Labor, was sent in by the Government to act as conciliator. *The Pinkertons, acting for General Motors, shadowed Mr. McGrady, a government officer.* It no longer surprises us to learn that spies trail John L. Lewis, Adolph Germer, Richard Frankensteen, and other leaders of labor; but this shadowing of a government officer while he is in the middle of his negotiations toward settlement of a strike, is a new angle. Yet the record leaves no room for doubt:

MR. MARTIN. [Pinkerton operative] . . . Mr. McGrady was pointed out to me by Mr. Brunswick. [Bronson, Burnside, now Brunswick.]

SENATOR THOMAS. Mr. Brunswick identified Mr. McGrady?

MR. MARTIN. Mr. Brunswick identified Mr. McGrady.

SENATOR THOMAS. And told you to follow McGrady?

MR. MARTIN. And told me to follow McGrady.

SENATOR THOMAS. For what purpose?

MR. MARTIN. When he came out to follow him, see where he went and whom he talked to.

. . .

SENATOR THOMAS. Then you did what?

MR. MARTIN. Then I was told by Mr. Brunswick to go to a room downstairs, that Mr. Brunswick had made arrangements with the manager of the hotel. This room was right next door to the one supposedly occupied by Mr. McGrady.

SENATOR THOMAS. That is, Mr. Brunswick knew the hotel in which McGrady lived?

MR. MARTIN. Yes.

SENATOR THOMAS. And he made arrangements for you to have the room next door?

MR. MARTIN. He made arrangements for us to have the room next door.

SENATOR THOMAS. So that you could shadow him?

MR. MARTIN. So we could sit in there and try to hear what they were talking about.

SENATOR THOMAS. In the next room?

MR. MARTIN. Yes, sir.

SENATOR THOMAS. What hotel was that?

MR. MARTIN. The Secor Hotel.

SENATOR THOMAS. Did you go to the room?

MR. MARTIN. We went to the room but did not hear anything.

SENATOR THOMAS. Well, you mean Mr. McGrady did not come into the room?

MR. MARTIN. I could not tell who was in the room. There was someone in there. Everything was mumbled; I could not even say Mr. McGrady was in there. He was supposed to be in there with these other men.

SENATOR THOMAS. They talked in low voices?

MR. MARTIN. Well, they talked loud enough, but you could not understand anything.

SENATOR THOMAS. They talked in a foreign language?

MR. MARTIN. No, sir.

SENATOR THOMAS. How did you try to understand it? Did you get near the transom?

MR. MARTIN. All we had to do was to get up near the wall. That is all I could do.

SENATOR THOMAS. Did you try that again?

MR. MARTIN. Well, on two or three occasions like that, always at night.

SENATOR THOMAS. Always at night?

MR. MARTIN. Always at night.

SENATOR THOMAS. When Mr. McGrady came home?

MR. MARTIN. Yes.

Martin's testimony was corroborated when Brunswick-Burnside was on the stand.

SENATOR THOMAS. Mr. McGrady's chief job was to try to settle strikes, was it not?

MR. BURNSIDE. Yes.

SENATOR THOMAS. Why would you want to shadow him?

MR. BURNSIDE. I presume, to see what his contacts were. I had those instructions from Mr. Clark, as I remember, to place him under surveillance. I presume it was to see who he was contacting, where he went.

. . .

SENATOR THOMAS. Could it possibly have been because you did not want to see the strike settled?

MR. BURNSIDE. No, sir.

SENATOR THOMAS. That you wanted to sell more of your wares?

MR. BURNSIDE. No, no.

SENATOR THOMAS. You know that there has been testimony given here that that has been done, do you not?

MR. BURNSIDE. So I understand.

SENATOR THOMAS. Did you know that Mr. McGrady was Assistant Secretary of Labor at the time you shadowed him?

MR. BURNSIDE. I do not believe I knew his exact title, Senator. I knew he was connected with the Labor Department; he was there as conciliator or mediator, or something of that kind.

SENATOR THOMAS. Would it be commonplace for you to accept a task like that, shadowing Government men?

MR. BURNSIDE. Well, in shadowing anyone, Senator, that a client, whom we considered responsible, had reason to take interest in, as to their movements and so on, if it appeared there was nothing unethical or nothing illogical about it, I presume we would take the job, whether they were Government officials or who they were.

SENATOR THOMAS. Do you think any of your employees had an idea which way Mr. McGrady's opinions would tend,

toward the right or toward the left, toward radicalism or
toward conservatism?

. . .

MR. BURNSIDE. Mr. McGrady, as far as I know, always had
a very fair reputation, a reputation as being fair, not being
inclined toward one side or the other. That is why he has been
so successful in settling a great many of these difficulties.

SENATOR THOMAS. If Mr. McGrady is such a fine man,
what about the ethics of eavesdropping, putting a couple of
men next to his room to listen?

MR. BURNSIDE. To try to, as Mr. Martin said, hear what was
going on in there, to see what progress was being made. If it
were for the holding company, [General Motors], for instance,
they might be interested in knowing how soon the thing was
coming to a settlement, so that they could make their plans
accordingly . . .

. . .

SENATOR THOMAS. In the Chevrolet strike in Toledo in 1935,
what information could be more important to General Motors
than to know what concessions the union would make, Mr.
Burnside?

MR. BURNSIDE. That would be important, yes.

SENATOR THOMAS. In other words, if you had gotten some information that you could have sent on to your employers in the
shadowing of Mr. McGrady, it would have been a trump card
in your espionage work, would it not?

MR. BURNSIDE. They might consider it so.

SENATOR THOMAS. It would very largely interfere with bringing about a settlement?

. . .

MR. BURNSIDE. It might have an effect.

SENATOR THOMAS. Well, Mr. Pinkerton, do you think so?

MR. PINKERTON. I do . . .

. . .

SENATOR THOMAS. . . . What about interfering with the
bringing about of peace? That is the aim of the conciliator. He

represents the public. He does not represent the strikers and he does not represent the concerns at all, but he represents the general public. Now, in that position he must have the absolute trust of both sides or else all his work is ineffective. The minute you spy on him you cannot do anything else but break down that trust.

MR. PINKERTON. If the fact is known it would have a bearing on it.

SENATOR THOMAS. To give an actual illustration, any evidence the union committee reveals of what it might concede, if through that, your General Motors, that is, your employer, learns that, it would be extremely valuable to General Motors; would it not?

. . .

MR. BURNSIDE. I presume it would.

SENATOR THOMAS. For example, put it in simple arithmetic: If the strikers are striking for a raise of 50 cents a day in the case, and the conciliator knows that they will accept 25 cents a day but the firm does not know it as yet but you find out that they would, would it not be the stupidest firm on earth that would not hold out for a saving of 25 cents?

MR. BURNSIDE. It would seem to me that if the conciliator knew that the 25 cents was a common meeting ground, that that would be the point to fix the settlement, anyway.

SENATOR THOMAS. Yes; but you have got that and you tell it to the persons on one side and they have got that information. Do you not see that you have given them a weapon whereby they will hold out and hold out until they [the strikers] break?

MR. BURNSIDE. I can conceive of that; yes.

In the McGrady case the Pinks admitted shadowing a government official. Still, in all fairness to them, it must be admitted that other evidence was introduced showing that they were prepared at any time to work not *on* but *for* government officials, if they were given the opportunity. This evidence was extremely interesting because to do so would have been a violation of a law passed on March 3, 1893. The law was a direct result of the major part played by the Pinkerton Agency in the bloody Homestead Strike. Congress, at that time, was so outraged by this employment of private detectives which resulted in ten deaths, that it passed the law prohibiting the Federal Government or any of its departments from ever employing detective agencies — and it mentioned the Pinkerton Agency specifically.

But a law passed by the Congress of the United States was a mere detail to be lightly brushed aside when the Pinks were after business. Detective agencies are on to every trick of the game when it comes to beating the law, and the Pinkertons are no exception. Order 106 of the Pinkerton Order Book is a gem in that it first quotes the law prohibiting the employment of the agency, and then goes on deliberately to show how that law can be evaded!

SENATOR LA FOLLETTE. I will read certain portions of . . . page 4 of Order 106 taken from the Pinkerton Order Book.

"13. United States Government.

(a) Act of March 3, 1893, Vol. #2. p. 121, Supp. R.S.U.S. provides 'That hereafter no employee of the Pinkerton's Detective Agency, or similar Agency, shall be employed in any Government Service, or by an officer of the District of Columbia . . .'

(b) Under this law the United States Government can refuse to pay Agency's bills.

(c) When solicited by United States officials, their attention should be called to this law and, if responsible, their personal guarantee for payment of our account secured, otherwise from some other responsible person.

(d) The law has been overcome by Government officials by our rendering to them two bills. One in the usual detail, the other on plain paper for the total amount for them to use as a voucher, as exampled:

John Smith (the official)
To Peter Doe (An agency clerk's name)
For services and expenses — $375.25
   (e) Reports should be rendered on plain paper, operative designated by number and not signed, and with no mention of the agency."
   Now, it is clearly the intent of that order, is it not, Mr. Pinkerton, to indicate methods of evading the law?
   MR. PINKERTON. Yes.

A detailed bill and a fake bill — the same technique that was in use for General Motors. Fool the workers in one case, fool the law in the other. (Note that there must be two sides to this illegal bargain — government officials on the one, Pinkertons on the other.)
   The Social Security Act which required that the names of employees be filed with the government authorities gave the agencies a real headache. Because secrecy is so essential to their business they felt that they must not reveal the names of their operatives. But the law said they must. What to do about it?
   There's always a way out for these slippery boys. They solved the problem by removing the operatives from their own payroll and having them appear only on the payroll of the corporations in which they were operating. Brilliant stroke, wasn't it? John Mohacsi, C.A.C. operative, tells how it worked in his case: "In and about January 4, 1937, I was called into the office by Stewart and I filled out a card resigning my position with the Int. Aux. Corp. I was then instructed to sign a new contract of employment for the handing in of reports to the Worthington Pump Company. I was to receive the same amount of pay but it would come directly from the Worthington Pump Company. All my reports and activities were to continue in the same way, being supervised by Stewart of the Int. Aux. Corp. and there was no change in the manner or place to which I was to send my reports."
   When Smith, C.A.C. president, was asked why his corporation had inaugurated this new practice this was his answer:

MR. SMITH. Oh, it is a question of the Social Security Act, I imagine.

SENATOR LA FOLLETTE. To relieve your corporation of the responsibility of reporting under the Social Security Act?

MR. SMITH. Yes.

State and city laws requiring registration of operatives were a nuisance. There were, of course, ways of getting around these laws, and in some states, some agencies pulled fast ones like that of C.A.C. on the Social Security Act. But occasionally the boys slipped — or else they just didn't bother to obey the law. The evidence shows that Railway Audit violated the Wisconsin law requiring registration of operatives; that Corporations Auxiliary "complied" with the Wisconsin law by a trick — but paid no attention to a similar law in the state of Indiana; that the Pinkerton Agency did not register at least one secret operative in Atlanta, where there was an ordinance requiring such registration.

In its returns to the men at the top, and in its hooking aspect, the spy industry has been likened to the business of organized prostitution. In its method of getting and keeping business the spy industry is like the armament industry.

In the United States one unique offshoot of the business of making armaments for warring nations is the business of making munitions, tear gas, and machine guns for industrialists for "plant protection" in case of strikes. This offshoot of the armament industry, like its parent, thrives on trouble. Business is best when the customer is scared. Orders roll in when the customer's security is threatened. Federal Laboratories, Inc., the Lake Erie Chemical Co., and the Manville Manufacturing Co., the three principal munitions makers for industrial use in the United States, are ever on the lookout for what they call "trouble" i.e., strikes.

So with the spy agencies. They too thrive on "trouble" — defined by them as "any attempt by workers to organize." Let a union organizer show his head in any locality and the salesmen for the spy agencies turn up at once soliciting business. The similarity is plainly illustrated in a comparison of letters from the munitions and spy agency salesmen. Mr. Herrick Foote, munitions salesman of New Haven, Conn., writes to Mr. A. S. Ailes, vice president of the Lake Erie Chemical Co. on April 5th, 1935. "I am doing a lot of missionary work in anticipation of a strike this spring, and I'm in a position to send in some good orders, if it will only mature. *Wish a hell of a strike would get under way.*" Two months later, he writes again as the situation gets hotter:

NEW HAVEN, CONN., June 15, 1935.

A. S. AILES,

Lake Erie Chemical Company, Cleveland, Ohio.

Dear Mr. Ailes: I beg to advise you that at a meeting of the national officials of the United Textile Workers Union of America held at Providence, R. I., yesterday demanded a 20% increase in wages for the workers in the cotton and woolen mills and if this 20% increase was not given within the next ten days, a general strike throughout the country would be called. This looks like some business and if this strike matures it will be a bad one. Hope you have something definite as to the new long range gun, as we will be in a bad way, if this strike gets under way and we have no long range guns . . . *I hope that this strike develops and matures and that it will be a damn bad one, we need the money* . . . Everyone wants to be up on their toes, watching this situation and work fast . . .

Very truly yours,

HERRICK FOOTE.

Just as Mr. Foote of the munitions industry saw business coming his way as a strike situation developed and matured, so Operative 423 (W. H. Gray, of Railway Audit) looked for business in Tennessee where, in July 1935, a number of A. F. of L. organizers had made their appearance. Mr. Gray of the spy agency was following Foote's prescription for the munitions men — he was on his toes, watching the situation, and working fast:

Att: 700 [Mr. L. D. Rice, vice-president and general manager]

7-24-35

I picked a Tenn. Labor Paper, and found that there is *considerable activity going on around Johnson City*, Tenn., as well as Knox[ville]; also *the Hosiery Workers are getting aroused in Nashville, Tenn. I will get to Johnson City* as soon as I can without haveing to make to long a jump . . . Mr. Temple showed me a letter from the Tenn. Mfg. Assoc; Sect. from Nashville, Tenn. and they are very much alarmed over there, as there Wash. Rep. [representative] reports that AFL. sent out 600 L:O [labor organizers] in the past two weeks, and plenty of them headed South, so I will get out of here to-morrow and *work to ward Nash. Tenn.* . . .

Yours Truly,

#423

How shall we mark Operative Gray's work?

Spelling.   40

Spotter of union activity.   100

Effort.   100

That both the munitions and the spy industries should be on the lookout for trouble areas where they could sell their services was to be expected. They are alike again in that when they are unsuccessful in their hunt for trouble — when the trouble they are looking for has not yet come to the surface — then they either make it or fake it. The story of how the armament makers stir up trouble, then profit from the trouble they have made, has been told repeatedly in books and pamphlets. But how do the spy agencies make trouble and profit from it?

Mr. Holderman, the hosiery union official who testified to an agency's unsuccessful attempt to hook him, tells how:

MR. HOLDERMAN. . . . He [the agency operative] then gave me instructions not only to mail in the reports on the union, to him, but also that I was to, as district manager, immediately tighten up on conditions in the Gotham Hosiery Co., which had a mill in Dover, N. J., and one in New York City, which, combined, employed about 1200 people.

SENATOR LA FOLLETTE. What did you understand him to mean when he said to "tighten up on them?"

MR. HOLDERMAN. *I was to go after increasing the wages and shorten the hours in behalf of the people there.* We subsequently checked up on why these instructions were given, and we found that *at the same time these instructions were issued to me the representative of the same company had approached the Gotham management.*

SENATOR LA FOLLETTE. You mean the same detective agency?

MR. HOLDERMAN. The same detective agency. *They approached the Gotham management and they told them that trouble was brewing in their Dover and New York plants and that they could solve their labor difficulties.*

SENATOR LA FOLLETTE. You mean that the detective agency could solve them?

MR. HOLDERMAN. The detective agency could solve these labor difficulties and prevent the trouble which was at that time pending.

Marvelous scheme, isn't it? The agency sends one of its spies into a plant through the back door to stir up trouble; then it sends one of its smooth salesmen through the front door to sell its services in putting down the very trouble that it has itself brewed! And a duped, frightened plant management usually falls for it!

This technique for getting business is so fantastic that it's almost unbelievable. But it's true. Take the word of Senator Wheeler of Montana. On April 7, 1937, on the floor of the Senate Chamber, Senator Wheeler said: "I have had a great deal of experience . . . with the industrial spy system . . . When I was a prosecuting attorney I had occasion to investigate some of these cases. I found that what would happen would be that industrial spies would get into a union and then would go out and try to get decent union men to commit some crime — to blow up a transformer, to put dynamite under a building, or blow up something — or they would drive nails into logs or set fire to mines and try to get decent men belonging to the unions to do these very things, *for the purpose of creating jobs for the spies' particular organization.* In two particular cases we had direct, positive evidence of this being done . . .

"As I said a moment ago, these spies would get into the union, and then would go out and create a situation whereby they would frighten the lawyers and the officers of the company to such an extent that they would have to employ a great many more men to watch these 'dangerous' men; and when the 'dangerous' literature that was being put out, or the suggestions that were being made by supposedly bad men, were traced down, they were almost invariably traced to the Pinkerton or the Burns or the Thiel detective who was lurking in the background."

Not only do spy agencies make trouble to get business, but they also fake trouble to keep the business once they have got it. Lyle Letteer, former Pinkerton operative, tells about the instructions he received on a job for General Motors, from Mr. Littlejohn, superintendent of the Atlanta office.

MR. LETTEER. . . . To use his expression, he said that my reports would have to have more meat in them.

. . .

SENATOR LA FOLLETTE. Did Mr. Littlejohn tell you why to make them meatier?

MR. LETTEER. He said he wanted to pull the investigation along.

SENATOR LA FOLLETTE. Wanted to what?

MR. LETTEER. Prolong the investigation.

SENATOR LA FOLLETTE. How did he say it would prolong it if you made your reports longer and meatier?

MR. LETTEER. He said if I made the reports longer and put more meat into them, that the Detroit office would carry them along quite a while longer than they ordinarily would run.

Littlejohn of Pinkerton's wasn't the only one who had this

bright idea. When Mr. Kuhl worked for National Corporation
Service, he gave the operatives under him the same cute advice:

SENATOR LA FOLLETTE. Did you ever assist in building up
jobs?

MR. KUHL. Well I did to this extent: To use the expression
that is used in these kind of companies, I have went out and
put the "heat" on.

SENATOR LA FOLLETTE. Just tell us about that.

MR. KUHL. For instance, an operative was falling back in his
work, or this client does not seem to think he is receiving
enough information, why, you go out and get hold of these
"ops" and tell them; come right out and tell them flat turkey,
"It is your job, too, so maybe *you better use your imagination a
little and write something in here that is of interest to the client.*"

This looks very much as though the agencies occasionally doublecross the employers who hire them. They do. As long ago as 1923,
that fact was plain to Roger W. Babson, who has made it his life
work to advise business men how to make money. In a special
bulletin to industrial leaders in that year, Mr. Babson solemnly
warned them against spy agencies. "There are a score or more of
these industrial spy agencies at work in the country. They act
under all kinds of names which give no hint of their real work. Im-
mense sums are paid to them by our employers.

"This is a serious blunder on the part of corporation leaders. It
stirs up trouble where none exists. It is the most potent breeder of
radicalism that we have . . . The 'boring from within' which radical agitators are charged with, is a drop in the bucket to the boring
that the industrial spy does for money which the employer pays.
These spy agencies set out to find rottenness, and if they do not
actually find it, some make it or fake it."

It is now fourteen years since Mr. Babson wrote this bitter attack
on one of the "services" the detective agencies perform for corporation leaders. At that time, strike-breaking was another agency
service paid for by industrialists. It still is. But the weapons used

in strike-breaking have changed — and as you can easily guess, the smart dick agencies have kept abreast of the times. Where formerly agency thugs would use only blackjacks, clubs, and bullets to break up a picket line, the 1937 model includes tear gas, vomiting gas, and the like. A sales circular of the Lake Erie Chemical Co. thus describes the effects produced by one of its nauseating gases: "Once rioters have been subdued with K.O. gas they will not invite another dose until their memory of the last experience becomes very dim, indeed. What does K.O. gas do to the victim?

"1. Violent nausea and vomiting.

"2. Sense of suffocation as if several men were sitting on chest.

"3. Intense pain in chest and head . . ."

This is actually one of the less harmful weapons now available to strike-breaking agency thugs. A more dangerous one, put out by the same company, is thus described in the sales circular: "The gas from the Green Band grenade is invisible making it more effective and terrifying, because it is not possible for the rioters to determine where the gas cloud begins or ends as is the case with all burning-type munitions." From another circular, describing the same weapon, we learn that "The grenade body tears into ribbons and these ribbons, together with firing mechanism, are thrown with considerable force in all directions from point of burst, with possible severe injury to persons within a radius of approximately fifteen feet thereof.

"This grenade should not be thrown into a crowd unless very severe treatment is necessary, as the pain from the high concentration of this gas in the eyes, nose and throat is almost unbearable. Unless drastic treatment is necessary, throw the grenade about 30 or 40 feet 'upwind' of the mob."

Pretty toys these, aren't they, to be put into the hands of strike-breaking agency operatives, many of them with criminal records a mile long! And that it often is the detective agencies which use such weapons is shown in part of a letter written by the secretary-treasurer of the Manville Manufacturing Co. to a salesman: "In regard to your questions, I will try and answer them as follows: Our equipment was used to break up the strike of the Ohio Rubber Company at Willoughby, Ohio, and to break up the strike in the Gear Plant of Toledo, Ohio; was used at the Eaton Axle plant at Cleveland, at the Real Silk Hosiery Company, of Indianapolis, and at a great many smaller places. In each of the above cases the equipment was used by the detective agencies brought in to protect the plant . . ."

Further proof. The following is particularly interesting because it brings to light the same kind of monkey business that we've met earlier — even more vividly. For here is a shipment of gas and munitions, etc., for the Firestone Tire Company, Akron, Ohio, which is shipped to a Joseph Folk, Lakewood, Ohio, part of it sent as a gift to a D. C. Graham, and billed to the Pinkerton agency!

SENATOR LA FOLLETTE. Will you look at exhibit 213, please, Mr. Ailes? Is this a copy of a work order of the Lake Erie Chemical Co.?

MR. AILES. It is, apparently.

SENATOR LA FOLLETTE. This is a work order of the Lake Erie Chemical Co. It shows a large number of various kinds of equipment: gas fountain pens, .410 caliber, serial number; Baby Giant gas projector; Baby Giant gas projector shells; watchmen's clubs; watchmen's club shells; gas riot pistols; gas riot pistol shells; hand grenades; Universal, Universal C N. What does "C N" refer to?

MR. AILES. Tear gas.

SENATOR LA FOLLETTE. And "D M"?

MR. AILES. Nauseating gas.

SENATOR LA FOLLETTE. L R field gun, L R shells. That is long range?

MR. AILES. Long range; yes.

SENATOR LA FOLLETTE. Band, candles, and so forth, warning label in shipment. One Baby Giant gas projector and three Baby Giant gas projector shells are marked as a gift to D. C. Graham. Do you know anything about that?

MR. AILES. I don't know about him.

SENATOR LA FOLLETTE. It says "For Firestone Tire, Akron, Ohio, ship to Joseph Folk, Lakewood, Ohio." Do you know who he is?

MR. AILES. I do not.

SENATOR LA FOLLETTE. And then it says, "Send or give bill to Pinkerton." What does that mean; that they are the people to be billed for the shipment?

MR. AILES. It probably means that, if they are to get the bill.

Mixed up as this transaction was, it was quite clear that the equipment was to be used at the Firestone plant. On another order, the Lake Erie Chemical Co. was not as frank about who the real purchaser of the equipment was. Look this bill over and try to determine who bought the goods:

July 11, 1935.
Sold to: W. H. Grabbe, 147 South 21st St. Terre Haute, Ind.
Shipped to: J. B. South c/o Railway Express Co.; Terre Haute Ind. via B/L 5354
    Express Paid

75 Universal tear gas candles, no. 1, series Nos. B-284, to 2903 and 3004 to 3015, $10.00......	$750.00
25 Universal K O & Lightning #5 candles, no. 2755 to 2779, $14.00........................	350.00
4 Long range field gun outfits complete, each consisting of —	
1 carrying case	
7 long range tear gas shells	
7 long range K O & tear gas shells	768.00
2 illuminating star shells	
4 long range field guns, nos. 1119, 1008, 1013, and 1018	
	$1868.00
Plus express paid.....................	14.02
	$1882.02

It looks as though this shipment of goods was sold to a Mr. W. H. Grabbe, doesn't it? Actually, the Columbian Stamping & Enameling Co. of Terre Haute was the real purchaser. This particular sale is of especial interest because the go-between in the transaction was Mr. Edgar E. MacGriffin, president of the National Corporation Service, a dick agency. MacGriffin got a commission of 20%, or $373.60 for arranging the sale. Thus we learn that not only do the agencies make use of the equipment of munitions firms on jobs which they are handling, but the tie is even closer — agency officials on occasion even act as salesmen for munitions firms.

In fact, the tie was so close in one case that the *spy agency and the munitions firm were one and the same*. The agency in question was Railway Audit and the munitions outfit was Federal Laboratories, Inc., the largest of the munitions firms. Mr. G. Eugene Ivey, whom we have met before as manager of the Atlanta office of Railway Audit, seems to have been a veritable Pooh-Bah; besides acting as manager, he was lawyer for Railway Audit — and at the same time he was District Manager of Federal Laboratories.

SENATOR LA FOLLETTE. How long were you district manager for them?

. . .

MR. IVEY. Only during the time that the Railway Audit Co. represented Federal Laboratories.

SENATOR LA FOLLETTE. And how long was that?

MR. IVEY. I believe about a year and a half.

SENATOR LA FOLLETTE. And during that time you were running the Federal Laboratories' business and the Railway Audit & Inspection Co.'s business at the same time?

MR. IVEY. Well, it was all one.

SENATOR LA FOLLETTE. Out of the Atlanta office?

MR. IVEY. Well, it was all one.

SENATOR LA FOLLETTE. It was all one?

MR. IVEY. Yes, sir.

What a pity that this intimate relationship existed for only a year and a half! However, the couple will be brought together again. It must be. So wonderful a marriage — the union of a detective agency with a munitions firm — cannot be broken permanently. The two partners have so much in common. Wedlock opens up possibilities that are breathtaking in their magnitude.

Think of it. A Spy Agency-Munitions Trust that could offer complete service from start to finish. What a chance! Just imagine how beautifully the *Union-Smashing Strike-Breaking Co. Inc.* could function. The Trust could be composed of four departments each one tying up with the other, and all working together harmoniously like a well oiled machine. In many cases, the industrialists will seek out the service. When that doesn't happen, then business can be worked up in some such manner:

1st. The Espionage Department plants a spy in Mr. Industrialist's factory to get the dope on any existing union activity — if there isn't any, he starts it going.

2nd. At the appropriate moment the Sales Division's slickest salesman approaches Mr. Industrialist and sells him USSBC industrial service.

3rd. A specially trained operative with a vivid imagination edits the spy's reports so they are "full of meat," with the usual effect: Mr. Industrialist is thrown into a panic of fear.

4th. A representative from the Munitions Section finds it a simple matter to sell the frightened Mr. Industrialist a load of munitions for "plant protection."

5th. Trouble. Either a strike is called by the union and its officials when the situation warrants it, or else the spy provokes an ill-advised strike.

6th. The Strike-Breaking Department immediately answers Mr. Industrialist's plea for assistance. Several hundred strikebreakers enter the plant.

7th. Mr. Industrialist's second and much larger order for munitions is quickly filled.

8th. A riot breaks out as the strike-breaking thugs attack the unarmed pickets with USSBC Fast-Flite shells and tear gas.

(*3 WORKERS KILLED, 14 WOUNDED*)

9th. The strike is broken.

10th. A crack salesman now convinces Mr. Industrialist that his greatest need is strike insurance. More spies and more munitions are brought to the plant, and the Strike-Breaking Department supplies a permanent staff of "plant police."

Such a scheme makes sense. How much more sensible that all these related services be supplied by one big company, e.g., The Union-Smashing Strike-Breaking Co. Inc., than that a lot of little separate firms be competing for the different parts of what is essentially one business. The Trust idea is not new. It has happened in other fields. Why not in this one?

The obvious first step is to find an experienced person with a genius for organization. Who will perform for this industry the organizing job which Rockefeller did for oil and Mellon for aluminum? The man who attempts it must have all the energy, cunning, and strength of our famous robber barons; he must be ruthless, dishonest, crafty, diabolical, corrupt, and lawless.

The encouraging thing is that the search for an individual with all these essential qualities need not be extensive. Most agency officials today can easily fill the bill.

VI. Employers Organize

We rarely hear, it has been said, of the combinations of masters; though frequently of those of workmen. But whoever imagines, upon this account, that masters rarely combine, is as ignorant of the world as of the subject. Masters are always and everywhere in a sort of tacit, but constant and uniform combination . . . We seldom, indeed, hear of this combination, because it is the usual, and one may say, the natural state of things which nobody ever hears of.

— ADAM SMITH, *Wealth of Nations*

THAT WAS WRITTEN in 1776, the year we declared our independence from England. What was true at that time is more than ever true today. With the rise of capitalist industry, combinations of employers have reached their highest development. In the United States more than 2,000 employers' associations have been organized.

Why? Professor Clarence E. Bonnett, in his *Employers' Associations in the United States*, a standard book on the subject, defines employers' associations and gives us the reason for their formation: "Any association, alliance, league or federation which intends to promote, directly or indirectly, *primarily the employers' interest in relation to labor*, is an employers' association."

Usually it's easy to spot an employers' association from its name. When you hear of the National Association of Manufacturers, or the Akron Employers' Association, or the National Metal Trades Association, you know at once what it is. If you read the speeches delivered at the meetings of the United States Chamber of Commerce or any of its local branches, the fact that they are employers' associations devoted to promoting employers' interests becomes plain immediately. You are, however, apt to be fooled by such names as the "Stark County Tax League," or the "Citizens' Alliance of Ramsey and Dakota Counties." These, too, are types of employers' associations just as any company union is. A good test is: who puts up the money. If employers' money is used to support an association, it's a safe bet that its purpose is to promote employers' interests.

Many employers in the United States feel that it is to their interest to crush genuine unionism. A major purpose of employers' associations, therefore, is to smash trade unions. It is no surprise to us to learn, then, that employers' associations are among the best clients of the dick agencies. W. Sherman Burns so informs all his office managers in a letter ordering them to solicit the business of some one hundred odd associations in every part of the country:

General Instructions
All Office Letter #704
Re: Soliciting, industrial work.

NEW YORK, July 28, 1936

To all offices:

Attached is a list of associations, their addresses, name of active officer and telephone number. This list was secured by Mr. Patterson of our Detroit Office, who received information at the time of securing this list that all of these organizations are very much interested in industrial undercover work and have a great deal to say in their respective territories, in an advisory capacity as to what industrial undercover service should be utilized by their members.

One of the principal functions of these associations and their officials is to make a study of the labor movement and to keep their members advised of all developments concerning their movement . . .

It is therefore suggested that each manager personally contact with the officials of these organizations in the cities where

United Automobile organizers show a friendly smile as Ford's service men advance grimly. The unionists are, left to right, Robert Cantor, Victor Reuther, Richard T. Frankensteen, and J. J. Kennedy   (*Pictures, Inc.*)

The muffled target in the center is Frankensteen, chief organizer for the Detroit district. The old guard tactic of pulling up the coat and then slugging is shown graphically here   *(Pictures, Inc.)*

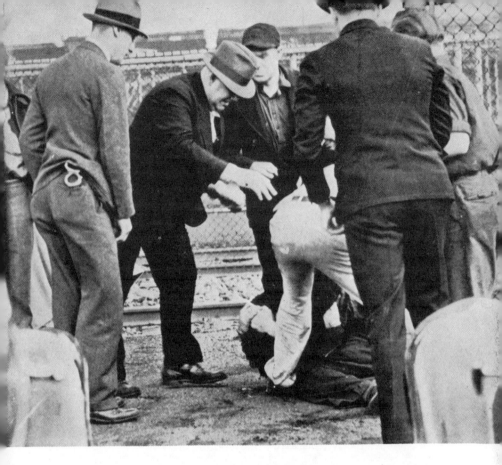

Down below — The Frankensteen battle took place on the overpass.
Guards go to work on another union man   (*Pictures, Inc.*)

"Memorial Day Massacre" at Republic Steel   (*Pictures, Inc.*)

our offices are located, and in other localities, contact by mail . . .

W. Sherman Burns

One of the names on the attached list was that of the "Employers Association of Akron, 500 Central Savings & Trust, Akron, Ohio . . . H. C. Parsons, Sec." The Burns man whose job it was to solicit business from Mr. Parsons was doomed to disappointment. A rival of the Burns agency, the Corporations Auxiliary Co., had had the business of this employers' association sewed up for over a quarter of a century. Mr. Parsons, on the stand, tells the story. It is a fascinating story. It shows, among other things, that four manufacturers of tires, in fierce competition with each other, were able to forget their business enmity and unite in an organization presenting a solid front against labor; rivals in business, friends in anti-labor activities. Nor did their association stand alone. It had a close connection with similar employers' associations throughout the country. A local union of manufacturers tied to a national union. In effect, an A. F. of M. — American Federation of Manufacturers. Adam Smith knew his stuff.

Here is Mr. Parsons testifying:

SENATOR LA FOLLETTE. What is your occupation, Mr. Parsons?

MR. PARSONS. I am secretary-treasurer of the Employers' Association of Akron.

. . .

SENATOR LA FOLLETTE. When was the Employers' Association formed, approximately?

MR. PARSONS. I think 1903.

SENATOR LA FOLLETTE. Who are the officers of the association at present?

MR. PARSONS. There is Mr. Slusser, of Goodyear; Mr. Pittinger, of Firestone . . . Mr. Charles Jahent, of General Tire . . . Mr. T. G. Graham, factory manager of the B. F. Goodrich Company.

SENATOR LA FOLLETTE. Are those all on the executive committee?

MR. PARSONS. That is all.

SENATOR LA FOLLETTE. The executive committee, then, is confined to representatives of the tire manufacturing companies in Akron?

MR. PARSONS. Yes; at the present time.

. . .

SENATOR LA FOLLETTE. How much do the companies pay to the Employers' Association each year?

. . .

MR. PARSONS. It formerly was 5 cents per employee and then was later raised to 8 cents, and more recently again to 5 cents. [A list of the members of the association and the amounts of their contributions, 1933–1936, is in Appendix D.–AUTHOR]

. . .

SENATOR LA FOLLETTE. What salary did you receive from the association, Mr. Parsons?

MR. PARSONS. $8,019 this last year.

SENATOR LA FOLLETTE. What are the chief items of expenditure of the association?

MR. PARSONS. The ordinary office expenditures, salaries, expenditures for special service.

SENATOR LA FOLLETTE. What do you mean by "special service"?

MR. PARSONS. The service of the Corporations Auxiliary Co.

SENATOR LA FOLLETTE. And how long have you had the service of Corporations Auxiliary?

MR. PARSONS. As I remember now, there were somewhat the same services there at the time I became secretary. [33 years ago]

SENATOR LA FOLLETTE. And it has continued throughout the time you have been secretary?

MR. PARSONS. Off and on, as I remember it; yes.

SENATOR LA FOLLETTE. Have the activities of labor organizers for outside unions had anything to do with the ebb and flow of your employment of Corporations Auxiliary?

MR. PARSONS. Yes.

SENATOR LA FOLLETTE. They have risen at times when organizational activity by outside unions was in progress?

MR. PARSONS. Yes.

SENATOR LA FOLLETTE. And fallen when they were not?

MR. PARSONS. That is about right . . .

. . .

SENATOR THOMAS. Do you attend annual meetings of other employers' organizations?

MR. PARSONS. Yes.

SENATOR THOMAS. What organizations are you affiliated with in that way?

MR. PARSONS. Well, we are not affiliated. I attend the meetings of the National Association of Manufacturers, the National Founders Association, on invitation, the National Metal Trades, and the National Industrial Conference. We are affiliated with the National Industrial Council.

. . .

SENATOR LA FOLLETTE. In 1936 I think the records you furnished the committee indicate that your costs for Corporations Auxiliary Service were approximately $21,000 . . . The total of your income in 1936 . . . was $36,000, and your own salary was $8,000; so it is a fair deduction, is it not, from these figures, that the bulk of the activities of the employers' association in Akron was devoted to labor espionage?

MR. PARSONS. I would not say the bulk of the activities, Senator; I would say the bulk of the expenditures.

. . .

SENATOR LA FOLLETTE. . . . The principal activity of the association aside from the work that you and your secretary did with the mimeograph and the meetings and the discussing of these various matters with representatives of the various companies that you have told us about, the principal and sole activity of the association outside of that was industrial espionage?

.   .   .

MR. PARSONS. Yes, that is true.

Now all this testimony of Mr. Parsons was very embarrassing to Mr. Paul W. Litchfield, the president of the Goodyear Tire and Rubber Co., who had testified the previous few minutes. His testimony had sounded sincere, straightforward — just what was to be expected of a great captain of industry. But before Parsons had gone very far it developed that Mr. Litchfield was as much of a twister as the other witnesses — perhaps a little worse. The pious flourish with which he began ended in a complete fizzle. Read the testimony and witness the collapse of the highly inflated Goodyear dirigible as it is brought down to earth.

SENATOR LA FOLLETTE. Mr. Litchfield, the committee would be interested in having your views on the use of labor espionage and strike-breaking agencies, if you would be so kind as to give them to us.

MR. LITCHFIELD. When I came with the company in its early days we had one or two operatives in the plant, which we carried on for several years. In 1913 when we began to grow, *my experience with that sort of thing was such that it led me to pass on a firm order that from 1913 on there would be no outside agencies, no espionage in the plant whatsoever; and I think that policy has been carried out.* We have not employed any outside agency of espionage or of strike-breaking organizations since I have been president of the factory, or manager of the company, so far as I know.

.   .   .

SENATOR LA FOLLETTE. Did you or did you not find that the use of industrial espionage tended to disrupt the good relations between employees and the employers?

MR. LITCHFIELD. We were inclined to that opinion.

Just the kind of forthright straight-from-the-shoulder statement that you would expect from the head of one of the greatest companies in the world. Mr. Litchfield felt that the spy system disrupted the good relations between boss and worker, so he firmly ordered that henceforth there was to be *"no espionage in the plant whatsoever."* So far so good. Our schoolboy faith in this great business leader is strengthened. Let us go on:

SENATOR LA FOLLETTE. As I understand it, the Goodyear Tire and Rubber Company is a member of the Akron Employers' Association; is that correct?

MR. LITCHFIELD. Yes; we are members of the Akron Employers' Association, the same as any trade association or any other kind of an association.

. . .

SENATOR LA FOLLETTE. And what is your understanding of the service that the association renders to your company and other members?

MR. LITCHFIELD. *It is just a general clearing house of information among the manufacturers.* I have never questioned very much as to what service it rendered, on account of the fact that we just belong, the same as we belong to any trade association, chamber of commerce, or anything else. We are assessed our *pro rata* share.

SENATOR LA FOLLETTE. Well, I assume that you must feel that the services rendered are worth while because of your contribution of $50,000 for 2 years — for 4 years, pardon me. Could you tell us in a little more detail what services the association rendered?

MR. LITCHFIELD. Well, so far as I know, the only thing that has come to my particular notice is statistics, from time to time, as to the number employed in each plant, and things of that nature.

. . .

SENATOR LA FOLLETTE. Are you familiar with the fact, Mr. Litchfield, that during the year 1936 the Akron Employers'

Association paid in excess of $21,000, or the bulk of its income to the Corporations Auxiliary Co. for industrial espionage?

MR. LITCHFIELD. I did not know that; no.

SENATOR LA FOLLETTE. And had you known it, would such an expenditure have met with your approval?

MR. LITCHFIELD. It would not so far as our plant is concerned. What they do outside we do not have anything to do with, in the management of that association.

SENATOR LA FOLLETTE. *Were you aware of the fact that the association had undercover men in your plant?*

MR. LITCHFIELD. *I was not aware of it.*

Nothing really wrong so far. It may be argued that Mr. Litchfield was showing bad judgment in paying out so much of his stockholders' money to an association which supplied his firm with nothing more than a kind of statistical service. That may be true. But on the absence of industrial espionage in his plant he still remains firm.

Then Parsons testified. Now look for Mr. Litchfield's about-face.

SENATOR LA FOLLETTE. Mr. Litchfield, were you a member of the executive committee of the association at any time?

MR. LITCHFIELD. I do not know whether it was the executive committee or what it was, but I was a representative of Goodyear many years ago, when I was factory manager, in the early days.

SENATOR LA FOLLETTE. Now, Mr. Litchfield, in order that the record may be complete, at the time you served on this executive committee, did you or did you not know of this arrangement that the association had with Corporations Auxiliary for undercover men?

MR. LITCHFIELD. *I think I did know that they did have that kind of an arrangement.*

. . .

SENATOR LA FOLLETTE. *During all the time that you were a representative of the Goodyear Company in this employers' asso-*

ciation you knew, did you not, that they were using undercover agents?

MR. LITCHFIELD. *I think that very likely I was aware of that fact.*

. . .

SENATOR LA FOLLETTE. Mr. Litchfield, I understood you, in response to a question by Senator Thomas, to say you never took any action while you were representing the Goodyear Company on the employers' association, to secure an abandonment of their use of industrial espionage technique; is that correct?

MR. LITCHFIELD. I do not recall I ever discussed that matter, except to state my disapproval of the practice. I do not think I ever pursued it any further.

SENATOR LA FOLLETTE. Did you make any effort after you assigned someone else to the work, to ascertain whether or not they had abandoned it?

MR. LITCHFIELD. No; I did not.

. . .

SENATOR LA FOLLETTE. And your company continued to contribute to the association and be a member of it?

MR. LITCHFIELD. We contributed to that association the same as a great many others, in that they were one of a large group and wanted a group to be a clearing house, but we never attempted to run the association.

SENATOR LA FOLLETTE. In the last 4 years you were paying out on the average of $17,000 a year to this association. *As far as your knowledge went, you did not know there had been any change in the policy of this association in the use of industrial espionage?*

MR. LITCHFIELD. *No.*

Turn back quickly to the opening brave speech of this witness. Seems like another fellow must have said those things, doesn't it? The Goodyear Tire and Rubber Co. was in partnership, through the Akron Employers' Association, with its biggest business rivals. The bond that united these competitors was the desire, common to all of them, to clamp down on the organizational activities of their workers. When the workers of the Goodyear Co. went out on strike in 1936, one of those miraculous "citizens' organizations" that spring up out of thin air to fight the strikers, suddenly made its appearance. The "Akron Law and Order League" was not a surprise to Mr. Litchfield. He knew it was going to be launched — in fact he had discussed its organization *with the presidents of Goodyear's competitors.* His own company contributed "something in the neighborhood of $15,000" to it.

Mr. Litchfield was listening in on the radio when former Mayor C. Nelson Sparks went on the air for recruits for the Law and Order League. What was the program of this citizens' organization? What did Mr. Litchfield hear the nurse of his $15,000 baby say? Keep the name of the organization in mind as you read the remarks Mayor Sparks made, after mentioning the names of John Brophy and several other representatives of labor organizations:

> *Help us to gang up* for constitutional law and order in this wonderful city. Help us to make this Law and Order League so representative of public opinion that we can say to those out-of-town radical leaders, who have lighted the fires of discontent in this city, to get the hell out of here, and *we are not going to be too much interested in the dignity of their going.*

This from the former mayor of the city, thè president of the Law and Order League! Small wonder that The Akron *Beacon-Journal* was alarmed. Its editorial for March 17th clearly pointed out that the Sparks' speech was a direct incitation to violence:

No Room for Vigilantes!

> The most ominous note yet sounded in the prolonged Goodyear strike is the call for recruits to a "Law and Order League." The name is a misnomer.
> Resort to organization of a "citizens' vigilante" to open the Goodyear Company plants is an open invitation to

rioting and violence. It is deliberately provocative and in-
flammatory. It will produce the exact opposite of law and
order . . .

The speeches of former Mayor C. Nelson Sparks, over the
radio Sunday, were unfortunate and ill-advised. He talked
loosely of driving leaders of the strike out of town, implying that typical vigilante mob methods might be in-
voked . . .

Unfortunately there was not a single note of calm
reasoned thinking in the speech. It was the typical product
of hysteria, when sanity is needed. It was incitation to
trouble, rather than an invitation to peace.

The Sparks move, *clearly endorsed by the Goodyear Company*, has evoked a warning from the strikers that violence
would be met with violence. Any man who stopped to
weigh the present tense situation would have known that
the counter-threat was inevitable . . .

If the Law and Order League does not at once abandon
its stupid and dangerous program, then Akron can prepare
itself for a bath of blood . . .

In the face of all this talk of violence, we renew our
appeal for sanity and right-thinking. We are thinking in
terms of human lives. We are thinking in terms of this
city's future. The idea that any group of citizens can take
the law into their own hands cannot be tolerated for a single
minute.

Let there be sanity and industrial peace, not madness
and war.

The italicized words in the foregoing quotation show that there
was no doubt in the editorial writer's mind as to who was behind
the Law and Order League. Nor should there be any doubt in your
mind as to who was behind the Flint Alliance that was so miraculously conceived in the General Motors strike; or the "John Q.
Public League" and similar "citizens' alliance" groups that
sprang up in the recent steel strike. They are all phoney. They are
dummy employers' organizations — the newest technique in
strike-breaking.

Convincing proof of this fact was furnished to the La Follette
Committee by Mr. E. T. Cunningham, in his testimony concerning
the RCA strike in Camden, N. J. in 1936. Mr. Cunningham, in
charge of labor relations for RCA, was impressed with a letter of

introduction from Governor Hoffman, presented by Max Sherwood of the Sherwood Detective Bureau. (The close relationship of many local, state, and government officials with the dick agencies is shameful.) Mr. Cunningham hired the Sherwood agency on the strength of the Hoffman introduction, plus the promises of Sherwood and his assistant, Williams. The description of the Sherwood technique is very revealing:

MR. CUNNINGHAM. . . . Both Sherwood and Williams stated that the old method of using strike-breakers and violence and things of that kind to win or combat a strike were things of the past; *that the way to win a strike was to organize community sentiment;* that they had been very successful in handling plans of that sort. They showed me enrollment slips — I cannot recall the exact title, but it was something like "Citizens' Welfare Committee" of such and such a city. They showed me a large full page ad, I believe from an Akron newspaper, in connection with a strike. They said they handled that. They sent men from door to door to get citizens to sign these membership slips, and if possible to get them to contribute to advertisements which would be run over the name of the so-called citizens' welfare organization, saying good things about the company and endeavoring in that way to promote a friendly public attitude to support the company. The details were a little more than that, but in substance that was the plan.

SENATOR LA FOLLETTE. Did he say, or did you gather from the newspaper advertisements and the blanks that he showed you, just what the citizens' committee was to do?

MR. CUNNINGHAM. Well, it was not clear, other than the favorable public reaction, throwing the weight to one's side as against the other; that is the only ——

SENATOR LA FOLLETTE. Did this Akron newspaper ad, as you remember, was it signed by a citizens' committee?

MR. CUNNINGHAM. Citizens' welfare committee, or something like that.

SENATOR LA FOLLETTE. Was the general effect of the advertisement to create the impression on the reader that the citizens' committee was taking the company side of the affair in Akron, so to speak?

MR. CUNNINGHAM. *Yes; and without any apparent identity with the company; it was to appear as an independent proposal as far as the public was concerned.*

SENATOR THOMAS. Did he show you any editorials that he thought he could have printed in the newspapers as a result of this advertising?

MR. CUNNINGHAM. There was something on that. My memory is not very good on just what he did show me, and I would not want to say exactly, but there was that impression, that editorials and news articles would be developed but that the *citizens would be organized to take the lead in the interest of the company and employment and they would organize that and the company apparently was not having anything to do with it.*

SENATOR THOMAS. You apparently got the impression his big job was to mold public sentiment?

MR. CUNNINGHAM. That was the impression. At the time, the strike was something new to me and I thought it was worth trying.

SENATOR THOMAS. He was to use the radio, newspapers, and house-to-house methods?

MR. CUNNINGHAM. Yes, sir.

SENATOR THOMAS. That is what they call missionary work in spy terminology; to take advantage of any opportunity to build public sentiment, feeling that pressure from without would probably do more good than work from within.

MR. CUNNINGHAM. Yes, sir; that was substantially my understanding.

SENATOR LA FOLLETTE. Mr. Cunningham, at this conference did they mention the fact that this might also be referred to as a law and order league, or something like that?

MR. CUNNINGHAM. Yes, sir. That was the main theme, now that you remind me; yes.

It should be clear from this testimony that those people who join the "back-to-work" movements, the vigilante committees, law and order leagues, etc. are the dupes of the strike-breaking dick agencies, hired by the employers.

Perhaps the most representative of employers' organizations in the United States is the National Metal Trades Association. Fortunately, we need no longer guess as to how it functions — we know now, because its officers were witnesses before the La Follette Committee.

The National Metal Trades Association on January 15, 1937, had a membership of 952 plants. It takes in those firms which employ machinists, coppersmiths, boilermakers, pipefitters, etc. — plants engaged in the manufacture of metals. The association began in 1899 with about forty members. Some of the well-known member firms are:

Chicago Branch
  Continental Can Co. (5 plants)
  Stewart Warner Corp.
Cleveland Branch
  Addressograph Multigraph Co.
  Warner & Swasey Co.
Detroit Branch
  Briggs Manufacturing Co.
  Chrysler Corp.
  Fisher Body Corp.
  Kelsey Hayes Wheel Co.
  Murray Corp. of America
  Timken Detroit Axle Co.
Grand Rapids Branch
  Grand Rapids Brass Co.

Kelvinator Co.
Hartford Branch
  United Aircraft Mfg. Co., Pratt & Whitney Div.
  Underwood Elliot Co.
Indianapolis Branch
  Chrysler Corp.
  Columbian Enameling & Stamping Co.
Milwaukee Branch
  Allis-Chalmers Mfg. Co.
  Cutler Hammer, Inc.
New York & New Jersey Branch
  Otis Elevator Co., Harrison
  Otis Elevator Co., Yonkers
  Wright Aero. Corp.

Rhode Island Branch	St. Louis Branch
Brown & Sharpe Mfg. Co.	Continental Can Co. (2 plants)
Morse Twist Drill & Mch. Co.	Wagner Elec. Corp.

The membership is based upon plants. Continental Can or Chrysler, for example, do not take out one membership for all their plants, but each plant 'takes out its own individual membership. The association has twenty-five local branches with headquarters in Chicago. Each of the branches employs a full-time staff.

Mr. Homer D. Sayre, the Commissioner of the association, is the chief active official. On the stand, he explained the purpose of the organization in terms strongly reminiscent of Smith, president of Corporations Auxiliary: ". . . The membership itself sees the need for the work of this association, which is the attempt to establish harmonious and mutual relations in the shops of its members, between its members and their employees . . . our primary interest . . . is to try and get the employer and employee to believe that their interests are mutual . . ."

Sounds familiar, doesn't it? The pious talk is familiar — and the method of establishing "harmonious relations" between the employer and employee whose "interests are mutual" is also familiar. For the National Metal Trades Association is not only an employers' get-together group; it is a spy agency and strike-breaking agency as well. It attains its harmonious relations by the usual method of union-smashing. It is a stout believer in the principle of the "open shop" — a shop open to non-union members only. It is very much concerned about the liberty and freedom of the workers in its member plants — it defends to the last these workers' inalienable right to choose not to belong to a real union. When these workers fall into error, when they show signs of exercising their equally inalienable right to join their own union, then the spies go to work, the men are quietly discharged, and harmonious relations are again restored. The union men, dubbed "agitators," are blacklisted and peace reigns in the N.M.T.A.

But even the best laid plans go wrong. Suppose this smooth-running machinery cracks up and the workers, in their blindness, forget for a moment that their interests and the boss's are mutual and go out on a strike. There is still no occasion to worry. The N.M.T.A. is prepared to meet the situation. Article XIII, Section 3, of its constitution gives assurance to the member plant that strike-breakers will be furnished up to seven-tenths of the number of workers for which the member has been paying dues. "In the case of a strike in the shop of a member, the Association may, upon request of the member, assist in procuring workers to replace the strikers; but the number of workers so procured shall not exceed seven-tenths of the number of striking employees covered by the member's regular assessment for the current quarter . . ."

Of course the member understands that for this protection he must be willing to bind himself to obey certain rules of the association. The N.M.T.A. is ready, willing, and able to swing into action on behalf of a stricken member, but he must agree to let them run the show. Article XIII, Sec. 1, makes that clear: "In the conduct of labor disputes members must proceed in the manner which the Constitution and By-Laws prescribe, failing in which they shall forfeit all right to the financial or moral support of the Association . . ."

Now what happens if a member calls upon the association to help fight a strike, and then either because he is lily-livered and can't stand seeing his workers attacked by the guards, or because he has come round to seeing that the strikers have just grievances, or because the strike is making him suffer heavy business losses, he decides to settle the strike? What happens? Can he meet with the men and end the dispute? Not on your life. It's not up to him. It's for the N.M.T.A. to decide if, when, and how a strike in this member plant shall be terminated: "Article XIII, Sec. 7, *Penalty for Settling Without Approval of Administrative Council.* If, without the consent of the Administrative Council, a member shall settle a difference or strike, the defense of which has been assumed by the Association, such member shall repay to the Association all the moneys which the Association may have expended on account of having assumed defense of such difference or strike, and shall also be liable to suspension or expulsion."

Does this seem a bit high handed? It isn't. It's a smart tactic. In fighting a war it's always best to have a unified command. The N.M.T.A. knows that in fighting for the employers against the workers, the safest and strongest procedure is a united front — collective action on the part of the employers. The workers have also learned that collective action is best. That's why they organize into unions. But what the N.M.T.A. wants for its own side, it is not at all willing to grant to the other side. Mr. Sayre was very reluctant to admit this, but judge for yourself:

SENATOR THOMAS. So that you have an organization which has all the possibilities of collective action on the part of the employers?

MR. SAYRE. Yes; I presume that is correct, in the preservation of the open shop.

SENATOR THOMAS. So that you have certain machinery set up that you can bring unity of stand, unity of action, unity of opinion about certain definite things?

. . .

MR. SAYRE. Yes; for the principle of the open shop that we stand for.

. . .

SENATOR THOMAS. If you take the words of your constitution, do not they mean this, that "We want collective action for ourselves and we want to forestall collective action on the part of the employees?"

MR. SAYRE. Well, that is not the policy of the association. We do not do that.

SENATOR THOMAS. In spite of what it says here?

MR. SAYRE. That is right.

SENATOR THOMAS. I am right in implying that from the words, am I not?

MR. SAYRE. Well, that would simply be an opinion. I do not think I would care to express an opinion on it.

SENATOR THOMAS. Well, has it not worked that way?

MR. SAYRE. No; it has not worked that way.

SENATOR THOMAS. Haven't you been more interested in keeping the employers on a collective-action basis than seeing that the employees get on a collective-action basis?

MR. SAYRE. Yes; in that respect that is correct.

What infinite patience was required to get these witnesses to give to words their obvious meaning! Mr. Sayre, like the dick agency officials and labor-relations directors of the big corporations, displayed amazing speed in spotting what labor was doing that his side didn't like, but he could seldom quite make the grade in discovering what his side was doing that labor didn't like. He didn't like to be helped either. And he certainly didn't enjoy Senator La Follette's and Senator Thomas's nasty habit of asking questions that would clarify some of his pretty speeches.

For example, Mr. Sayre proclaims, ". . . I think, generally speaking, the employers throughout the country are willing at any time to deal with their employees, either individually or collectively. What many of them object to is to dealing with outside representatives."

Now see what the questioning brought out in regard to that beautiful sentiment:

SENATOR THOMAS. What do you mean by outside representatives?

MR. SAYRE. Well, I mean business agents of a union and men of that description, that are not employed by the company.

SENATOR THOMAS. *Would not your organization be an outside agency from the employees' standpoint?*

MR. SAYRE. *I presume that is correct.*

. . .

SENATOR THOMAS. What if an employee organization should be set up and they should make the charge that they are against

the closed shop theory in regard to the employers; would that
not put your organization right out of existence?

MR. SAYRE. It might, if the employers agreed to that.

Commissioner Sayre got into other difficulties. Not only did he
have to admit that his organization was just as much an "outside
agency" as the business agents of a union were, but he had to
admit further that the N.M.T.A. was opposed to its members
making collective bargaining agreements. He had been stoutly
maintaining that the association was not opposed to its members
employing union workers, but that it was opposed to its members
signing closed shop agreements with unions. Under Senator La
Follette's questioning he had to concede that the N.M.T.A. was
opposed to its members signing even collective bargaining agreements. This admission came hard, but it came.

> SENATOR LA FOLLETTE. In other words, when you say you
> are opposed to a closed shop, what you really mean, if I under-
> stand you, is that you are opposed to any collective bargaining
> whereby the majority of the employees are designated as rep-
> resentatives of all of the employees for the purpose of signing
> an agreement, which affects the working conditions, the hours,
> and the wages of all the employees in the plant; is that not a
> fair statement?
>
> MR. SAYRE. Well, we are opposed —
>
> SENATOR LA FOLLETTE. (interrupting) No; I say, is that not a
> fair statement?
>
> MR. SAYRE. I do not want to make a mistake on it.
>
> SENATOR LA FOLLETTE. I do not want you to make any mis-
> take.
>
> MR. SAYRE. That is the point. I want to be perfectly honest
> in the thing. As I said, we are opposed to the closed shop,
> Senator.
>
> SENATOR LA FOLLETTE. You have said that a good many
> times and I understand all about that, but I understood from
> your testimony that what you regarded as a closed shop was

an agreement entered into between the employees, that no one in that shop could be employed who did not belong to a particular union. Is that correct?

MR. SAYRE. That is correct.

SENATOR LA FOLLETTE. All right. Now I am anxious to get your honest, straight-forward opinion . . . of a different situation, not a closed shop in the sense that all employees have to belong to a particular union, but a shop in which the employer recognizes the right of a majority of his employees to represent all of the employees in the plant, regardless of whether they belong to a union or not, for the purpose of entering into a contractual relation between the employees and the employer affecting hours, wages, and working conditions, and other things of interest to the employees.

MR. SAYRE. Well, we would probably say to that company that we felt that such an agreement was not justice to the minority, and would suggest that when the time came for renewing the agreement again that he should take that into consideration. I do not think, I am quite sure, the association would expel a company for that.

SENATOR LA FOLLETTE. . . . Do you know of any member of your association that has the kind of collective bargaining agreement that I described in my previous question?

MR. SAYRE. I do not recall offhand.

. . .

SENATOR LA FOLLETTE. You would be very disturbed, would you not, if one or several members of your association began to enter into the kind of agreements that I have suggested?

MR. SAYRE. Yes; I would.

SENATOR LA FOLLETTE. And you would bring it to the attention of the administrative executive council?

MR. SAYRE: Yes; I would; yes, sir.

SENATOR LA FOLLETTE. Do you not think the executive council would be disturbed about it?

MR. SAYRE. I think it would.

SENATOR LA FOLLETTE. All right. I think we understand each other, Mr. Sayre.

In the record there is an example of just such a case. Only Mr. Sayre did not need to refer the matter to the administrative executive council. He prevented the signing of the agreement between the N.M.T.A. member and the union by smashing the union. Follow the sequence of steps:

On April 25, 1934, the workers in the Morse Twist Drill & Machine Co. of New Bedford, Mass. (member of the N.M.T.A.) held an election under the auspices of the National Labor Relations Board, to determine who should represent them in collective bargaining with the company.

On April 27, 1934, the result of the election was communicated to the company by the N.L.R.B.:

April 27, 1934

MORSE TWIST DRILL & MACHINE CO.,
    New Bedford, Mass.

Gentlemen: The results of the election held by this Board for the employees of the Morse Twist Drill & Machine Co., held in New Bedford on April 25, 1934, for the purpose of determining who shall represent the employees in collective bargaining are as follows:

American Federation of Labor representatives 272
Local shop committee........................ 10
Miscellaneous............................... 2
                                            ——
    Total ballots cast........................ 284

We enclose a copy of the President's Executive order of February 1, 1934, as amended of February 23, 1934.

Yours very truly,
S. C. BARTLETT, JR.,
Executive Secretary.

The National Labor Relations Board officials carried out their instructions according to law. They held and properly supervised an election in the Morse Twist Drill Co. plant. They notified the company of the result. The next step should have been the signing of a collective bargaining agreement between the company and the union which had been elected by the workers to represent them.

But there is more than one way of skinning a cat.

All was not lost, not by a long shot. The N.M.T.A. could fix things up. No one can sign an agreement with a union that doesn't exist. So —

On April 28, 1934, application for a post office box in New Bedford was filed by Mr. George Lichtenberger. He was assigned Box No. 152.

Mr. George Lichtenberger was a spy — Operative 187 — in the employ of the N.M.T.A. He was sent in with orders to smash the union. He succeeded, according to the affidavit of a man who was in a position to know, Ferdinand Sylvia, A. F. of L. organizer:

> *Both the Revere Brass and the Morse Twist Drill unions with* *which Lichtenberger was identified have disintegrated . . .* I believe that in both these cases the real destructive influence was the action and attitude of Lichtenberger, particularly in the Morse Twist Drill where I had organized 127 members with full initiation fees and with the prospects of a potential organization of more than 500 members and where we had immediate success in raising wages and in securing recognition for purposes of collective bargaining through a national labor board election. Because of his influential position in the local and as a delegate to the New Bedford Central Labor Union, Lichtenberger was able to demoralize the members and the prospective members of the Morse Twist Drill Local by discrediting the organizers and by his efforts within the organization.
>
> FERDINAND SYLVIA.

Neat work, wasn't it? The N.M.T.A. officials were not boasting when they advised their own and prospective members that the association's "Private Detective Service" offered many advan-

tages over the industrial service of the ordinary spy agencies.
According to Mr. E. C. Davison, Mayor of Alexandria, and secre-
tary-treasurer of the International Association of Machinists, the
N.M.T.A. could be proud of the activities of its undercover men:

> MR. DAVISON. . . . In 1901 they became very active and
> began the process of placing in our organization undercover
> men, stool-pigeons, for the purpose of framing the officials
> of the organization, both local and international — our trou-
> ıbles were continuous.
>
> SENATOR LA FOLLETTE. What do you mean by "framing"?
>
> MR. DAVISON. By getting them into positions that are, I
> would say, unbearable; destroying their homes, if possible, by
> anonymous letters, many of which I have myself received in
> my earlier days, writing to our wives that we were familiar
> with other women, writing letters signing the names of women
> that would be sent to our homes, addressed to us, knowing full
> well that most of our wives take care of our mail at home . . .

There's a tactic which even the dick agencies wouldn't stoop to.
The N.M.T.A. spies know the advantage of becoming officials
in the union. When James Matles, grand lodge representative of
the International Association of Machinists, was shown a list of
the undercover operatives of the N.M.T.A. and the places where
they had worked, he recognized some of them as important union
officials: "I see the name of Ernest Goetz, Operator 249, Otis
Elevator, Yonkers, Worthington Pump, Ford Instrument Co., at
which company he is employed now; he is a member of Lodge 295,
Long Island City; he holds the office of trustee at the present time
. . . I see the name further on of Arthur Brook, Operator 433,
Silver & Pewter Manufacturers Association, New York, and later
as general operator. He is at present a member of the executive
board of Lodge 416 in Brooklyn . . . I see here also one other
important man. His name is A. W. Allten, Operative 479, the
Wright Aeronautical Co., Paterson, N. J. This man is holding office
now as secretary of the lodge and has all the records of every single

member working in Wright's. He is president of the State conference of the International Association of Machinists, a conference representing 12 or 14 lodges in that state."

Members of the N.M.T.A. are assured that their every request for aid in case of "trouble" (union activity) will be given prompt consideration. In April 1935 the Sunbeam Electric Co. of Evansville needed help. The reason is given in a letter from the secretary of the St. Louis Branch of the association to the national secretary:

. . . Of their [Sunbeam Electric Co.] employees who belong to this federal union, three are particularly active and pernicious. The company would like to get rid of these three men and *if you can suggest any way that they can accomplish this without laying themselves liable to a charge before the Regional Labor Board,* they would appreciate it very much. All three of them are very careful to do their work in such a way that it will not be possible to discharge them on those grounds and *their union activities are carried on outside the plant and in union meetings* . . . Mr. Schroeder believes that the interests of the firm require their immediate dismissal. *How can it be done?*

Did this employers' association, run by the high-minded Mr. Sayre, refuse indignantly to assist the Sunbeam Electric Co. violate the law? It did not. Did the N.M.T.A. write to the Sunbeam Electric Co. that its employees had a perfect right to do what they were doing? It did not. It came to the aid of its stricken member — Operative 116 was assigned to the case.

The N.M.T.A. is prepared to give to its members strike-breaking and "guard" service as well as spy service. In 1936 it had a "defense fund" of over $200,000 to use for strike-breaking purposes. (Incidentally, it paid no taxes on this war chest, because it is a "voluntary association.") Any outfit that is in the strike-breaking business is of great interest to the munitions firms. Mr. Ailes, vice-president of the Lake Erie Chemical Co. recognized that fact. On May 28, 1936, he wrote to one of his agents:

Dear Northcott: You will recall that I wrote to you several times about the National Metal Trades Association with headquarters in Chicago. *This outfit is a great potential source of business,* and I think we have overlooked a bet in not getting better acquainted with them . . .

They have a membership consisting of the most prominent metal-working concerns in the U. S.

I did not know until recently that *this concern furnished guards, strike-breakers, and the like for industrial concerns belonging to their association.* However, they do so, and dictate the defensive sources or materials that the members should buy . . .

Mr. Ailes was not a moment too soon. For at the very moment he was writing his letter, a strike was in progress at the Black & Decker Electric Co. of Kent, Ohio. This was a member firm of the N.M.T.A. and Mr. Ailes succeeded in "getting better acquainted" just in the nick of time. On June 18, the association's "guards" put into use the Lake Erie Chemical Co.'s products. Here is the story from the sworn testimony of Mr. C. A. Gadd, business representative for the International Association of Machinists:

SENATOR LA FOLLETTE. State the circumstances that led to the violence.

MR. GADD. Two trucks drove up there at 6 o'clock in the morning and crashed through the gate, men jumped out of them with sawed-off shotguns and tear gas guns.

SENATOR LA FOLLETTE. Approximately how many men were in the trucks? Do you remember?

MR. GADD. Well there were forty-some. I was under the impression there were forty nine of them altogether. They started shooting tear gas and shooting with the shotguns. They had some of the pickets that were suffering from gas taken to the hospital. One picket was shot in the right leg, gassed, and some of the other pickets were slightly wounded. One, by the name of Gray, was shot in the face with some buckshot . . .

SENATOR LA FOLLETTE. Were any women hurt?

MR. GADD. Yes, sir. There was a Mrs. Broffman . . . She had a gas shell explode right at her feet. She is still suffering from the effects of it [7 months after the shooting!–AUTHOR] . . .

· · ·

SENATOR LA FOLLETTE. Were there munitions found in the plant?

MR. GADD. Yes, sir.

SENATOR LA FOLLETTE. What kind of munitions?

MR. GADD. There were five sawed-off shotguns, five tear gas guns, long range guns, one full case and one part of a case of long range tear gas shells; there was quite a quantity of small arms ammunition, shotgun shells, and there were about a bushel basket full of revolvers and automatic pistols.

· · ·

SENATOR LA FOLLETTE. In the course of your negotiations for the agreement which was entered into subsequent to the removal of the guards, did you have any discussion with Mr. Lamb about the hiring of the guards?

MR. GADD. After the agreement was signed he said he did not hire any guards, that they turned the settlement of the strike over to the agency. He did not name the agency at that time.

SENATOR LA FOLLETTE. It has been developed in the testimony that it was the National Metal Trades Association.

MR. GADD. That is right.

Though Mr. Sayre explained at the beginning of his testimony that the purpose of the association was "to establish harmonious relations" between employers and employees, the complete record in no sense bears him out. As a matter of fact, when N.M.T.A. officials met with any employer who did try to establish peaceful relations with unionized workers, they did everything they could to change his point of view. Two cases from the record illustrate this point.

The first concerns Mr. George E. Deming, vice president of the

Philco Radio Co. of Philadelphia. Mr. Deming, it appears, did not stop with making pretty speeches about workers having the right to belong to unions of their own choosing, but he actually believed it — and his company signed an agreement with the union. That, in itself, would have made him an object of scorn to N.M.T.A. officials. But that wasn't all. Mr. Deming happened to be the employer-member of the mayor's labor committee and dared to stick to the position that other employers should sign agreements with the unions. That was more than Mr. L. A. Stringham, head of the N. Y. branch office of the N.M.T.A., could stand. He was indignant, and on March 8, 1936, wrote to Commissioner Sayre for advice. Part of that letter reads: "Deming is the best thing the A. F. of L. has in Philadelphia, and his constant agitation in favor of the A. F. of L. is adding strength to the organized labor movement.

"*This man should be broken down. Can you suggest anything that we can do to offset his activities?*"

Four days later came the Commissioner's answer, short and to the point:

Dear Mr. Stringham: The next time you see Mr. Kellèr I would suggest that you give him the benefit of your opinion regarding Mr. Deming's attitude on labor problems.

That is Mr. Sayre's advice in answer to Stringham's request for a method of "breaking down" Mr. Deming, the employer-friend of labor. It doesn't make sense until you understand that one of Philco's chief customers was the Chrysler Corporation, that Walter Chrysler was a stockholder in the Philco Co., *and that Mr. Keller was the President of the Chrysler Corporation.*

Get it? Mr. Deming, vice president of the Philco Co., dared to believe that labor had the right to organize and bargain collectively. He was to be "broken down" by having pressure brought to bear on him through Mr. Keller of Chrysler, one of his biggest customers.

Commissioner Sayre evidently knew all the tricks of the game, didn't he?

The second case is similar. A solicitor for an employers' open shop organization in Cleveland, tried to enroll Mr. Frank W. Caldwell, a dealer in Dodge cars there. Imagine his surprise and disgust at learning from Mr. Caldwell that he believed in collective bargaining, and that he had signed an agreement with his employees' union! The N.M.T.A. learned about Mr. Caldwell. Though it wasn't any of their business since Mr. Caldwell was not eligible for membership in the N.M.T.A.; nevertheless Mr. Sayre evidently thought Mr. Caldwell's condition was serious, and he proposed a remedy. He took the trouble to write a letter to Mr. Keller telling him about the attitude toward labor of Mr. Caldwell, the Dodge dealer who sold cars *made by the Chrysler Corporation*. It was indeed fortunate for the Chrysler Corporation that Commissioner Sayre didn't spot many more pro-labor employers with Chrysler connections, else President Keller would have had a full-time job just bringing pressure to bear where Sayre thought it was needed.

If a small Dodge dealer could arouse Commissioner Sayre so much, just imagine how his heart must have sunk, when he learned that Gerard Swope, Chairman of the Board of the great General Electric Company, was making eyes at unions! The horrible news came from the faithful Stringham in a report on an interview with Mr. Hinds of the Crouse Hinds Company, makers of electric signals.

> Mr. Hinds said that Mr. Crouse had evidently fallen for some of the talk he had heard coming from Girard Swope, of the General Electric Company, who was attempting to eliminate from industry the National Association of Manufacturers, the National Founders Association, and N.M.T.A. [that must have taken Sayre's breath away!—AUTHOR] That at a meeting in New York of the N.E.M.A. a couple of weeks ago, Swope attacked the above three associations; said they were out of the picture now, and could not do anything since 7-A [of the National Industrial Recovery Act] and the Labor Boards were instituted; that there was no need of them any more; that every one would

have to go along with the President from now on, and follow out his policies, etc. Manufacturers and members of the N.E.M.A. who were also in the three associations referred to, would not have to pay any more dues, but go along with the President and save their money.

Mr. Hinds agrees *that Swope is a dangerous man for industry;* that his wife, a former pal of Jane Adams of the Hull House, is active with him in their parlor pink activities.

Later on in the evening, conferred with our Syracuse correspondent and he informed me that he had just received a letter from Schenectady which advised him of a meeting . . . held in the General Electric office building, attended by the district officers of the four lodges of the International Association of Machinists, Schenectady, and was presided over by Girard Swope and George Bowen of the I.A.M.

Here again the record is clear. Mr. Swope's wife was a pal of Jane Adams — mark him as "a parlor pink"; Mr. Swope believed in negotiating with trade unions — mark him as "a dangerous man for industry." We don't know whether Commissioner Sayre tried his usual tactic of communicating with President Keller of the Chrysler Corporation in this instance; we do know from another letter in the record that he expected to "make good use of the information" that Stringham had given him.

To what fantastic lengths the imagination of an employers' group runs when it meets an industrialist who deals with the union of his employees, is beautifully illustrated from another Stringham-to-Sayre letter. It is dated January 2, 1935, and part of it reads:

> . . . Counsel for the manufacturers and associations, during their deliberations, woke to the fact that there was a leak among their own group and through an investigation it is said that *Gerard Swope was not only informant for the other side of the fence* but was keeping them thoroughly advised and alive to everything that went on in the manufacturers' meetings.

A pretty spectacle! The major officials of one of the leading employers' associations in the U. S. labelling Gerard Swope, head of the General Electric Co., an informant! Perhaps the explanation lies in the fact that they themselves are so used to the employment of spies that they suspect everybody else, particularly an employer who so far forgets his position as to respect the rights of his employees to bargain collectively.

Another organization of employers which deserves attention is the National Association of Manufacturers, which one of its officers has described as "the most powerful body of business men which has ever been organized in any land, or in any age." The N.A.M. has in the U. S. over five thousand active and associate members; it has as affiliates over thirty state and several hundred local manufacturers' organizations, as well as many national trade associations.

Like the N.M.T.A., it states, as one of its purposes "the betterment of the relations between employer and employee," but its program for fulfilling that aim is quite different. It is not, directly, a spy and strike-breaking agency. It concerns itself instead, with the relations between business and government, and centers much of its attention on legislation — opposing those measures which threaten the power of business, and supporting (often helping to initiate) those measures which favor business. It concerns itself, too, with the shaping of public opinion in regard to industry.

For that job it is extremely well equipped. It has a treasury large enough to enable its Public Relations Committee to make extensive use of every propaganda medium in the country. At the annual convention of the N.A.M. on December 8, 1936, the chairman of the committee, Mr. Harry A. Bullis, gave the following report of the widespread activities of his committee in carrying industry's message to every American home.

The Press

Industrial Press Service — reaches 5300 weekly newspapers every week.

Weekly cartoon service — sent to 2000 weekly newspapers.

"Uncle Abner Says" — comic cartoon appearing in 309 daily papers with a total circulation of 2,000,000 readers.

"You and Your Nation's Affairs" — daily articles by well-known economists appearing in 260 newspapers with a total circulation of over 4,500,000.

Factual bulletin — monthly exposition of industry's viewpoint sent to every newspaper editor in the country.

For foreign-born citizens — weekly press service, translated into German, Hungarian, Polish, and Italian, printed in papers with a total circulation of almost 2,500,000.

Nation-wide advertising — 6 full page ads about the "American System," of which over 500 newspapers have carried one or more.

The Radio

"The American Family Robinson" — program heard from coast to coast over 222 radio stations once a week, and over 176 stations twice a week.

Foreign language — 1188 programs in 6 languages over 79 radio stations.

The Movies

Two 10-minute films for general distribution, seen by over 2,000,000 people.

Public Meetings

70 meetings featuring 8 professional speakers.

Employee Information Service

Leaflets — a series of 25 distributed to over 11,000,000 workers.

Posters — over 300,000 of a series of 24 for bulletin boards in plants throughout the country.

Films — 10 sound slide films for showing in plants.

Outdoor advertising

60,000 billboard ads scheduled for 1937.

Pamphlets
"You and Industry Library" — over 1,000,000 copies of a
series of seven pamphlets distributed to libraries, colleges,
business men, lawyers, and educators.

Mr. Bullis admitted that when he himself contemplated the scope
of the N.A.M. public relations program, it took his breath away.
He told the convention, "I am always amazed at its completeness
and the way in which it reaches into every section of the country
and all strata of society."

Of the truth of that statement there can be no doubt.

Both the N.M.T.A. and the N.A.M. are big well known employers' organizations with a fairly open membership. There is another
type of combination of employers which is small, more or less
secretive, with restricted membership. An outstanding example of
such a group is the "special conference committee," which meets
once a month in the office of its secretary, Mr. E. S. Cowdrick, on
the 24th floor of Radio City. The personnel men of a group of select
important corporations make up this committee. The corporations
are world-famous: General Motors, Standard Oil Co. of New Jersey,
U. S. Rubber Co., U. S. Steel, Bethlehem Steel, International
Harvester, A. T. & T., Goodyear Tire & Rubber, Irving Trust Co.,
Du Pont Co., General Electric, and Westinghouse. No more. Each
corporation, if not the greatest in its field, is certainly one of the
greatest.

Several members of the group were on the stand before the La
Follette committee. They testified that the principal order of business at the monthly meetings was a presentation by each member
of a *résumé* of business conditions of his company and of the labor
situation; legislation such as 7-A of N.I.R.A. and the Social Security
Act was also discussed. Minutes of each meeting were kept and sent
to the members of the committee, but the three General Motors
witnesses who testified said that they had destroyed their copies.
The questioning did bring out, however, that this conference committee, while presumably merely a discussion group, became, in

effect, a common policy-making group; i.e., in the pooling of common experiences on labor-relations, the successful technique of one firm could be adopted by the others. This was true of company unions — *every corporation represented had a company union.*

Similarly, one member might report on the successful method his company used to put over salary reductions, and the other members would probably try to institute the same procedure in their plants. Mr. Hale of General Motors told how impressed he had been at hearing Joe Larkin, Bethlehem Steel Committee member, describe a clever method of bringing strong union men into line:

> I think it was in connection with one of the subsidiaries of Bethlehem Steel, if I remember; it was the Fall River Ship-building Co. where they had several very antagonistic men elected to the works council, very strong union men, you might say, and inclined to be — we might use the term broadly — radical in their views, and the point was brought out there that when they got them into the picture and these men had an opportunity, through that medium, to see some of the company's problems, how they were going at things, that they became supporters for the company's policies. I remember that particular discussion.

This kind of learning from the other fellow's experience is usual — we all do it. It was to be expected that these labor-relations directors of different large corporations, faced with the same problems, would join together to discuss those problems and their solution. (Look at a Goodyear letter to Mr. Cowdrick, Appendix E, for an example of how full the members' reports to the committee were.) Similarly, it was to be expected that a group of open shop employers, desirous of keeping unionism out of their plants, would join together in an organization like the N.M.T.A.; nor need anyone be surprised that manufacturers the country over, hoping to present a united front on legislative and labor matters, would join together in a powerful propaganda organization like the N.A.M. The fact that employers organize was not a surprise to Adam Smith way back in 1776. It should not be a surprise to us.

Employers are staunch believers in organization — for themselves. They not only believe in it — they practice it. Remember that, the next time you read about the fight they wage against trade unions, the organizations of the workers.

VII. "The American Way"

NOW LET'S STOP to look at the picture.

Workers in plants throughout the United States want to form unions and bargain collectively. They want to organize. Industrialists in plants throughout the United States also want to organize. They do. Nobody stops them. But these same industrialists are opposed to the efforts of their workers to organize and bargain collectively. The industrialists do not oppose unionization in word, but they do in deed. Spies are hired by the industrialists to help them in their fight against trade unions.

What is a spy? Let us turn to the *Oxford Dictionary*. "*spy* — a person employed in time of war to obtain secret information regarding the enemy." Spy is a war term. And labor spies are part of the industrial war. Understand, the opponents in this war are not the workers on the one side and the detective agencies on the other. Not at all. The detective agencies are the tools of the employers. They are paid by the employers. They would play no part in the war unless they were hired to do so. The line-up in this war is employers vs. workers, Capital vs. Labor.

Richard Frankensteen, on the stand before the La Follette committee, made the point that the people to blame for the spy system were not the spies, but the employers who hired them: "I would like to make this observation. I at one time listened in on a trial before Judge Moinet, a Federal judge in Detroit, and he had on trial a narcotic salesman, and he pointed out this man was not a dope-taker, and he said to this man, 'I am going to give you the highest penalty that the law allows me to give, because I think *you are much worse than the man who takes dope*, than the average addict, because he is a weak man.'

"I think men who pose as decent citizens, men like Weckler [vice-president of De Soto Motor Corporation, Chrysler subsidiary –AUTHOR] and K. T. Keller, *men of that type are in the same category as that dope salesman* . . . I want to say that the type of men that are hired for these spy jobs are the lowest type of criminals that you can find. Many of them have criminal records a mile long, and yet the same corporations, *Mr. Keller, Mr. Weckler, and the rest of them, hire these men and still* walk around as decent citizens, and I say they are not."

Of course the dick agencies are not free from blame. We have seen that in carrying out their business of union-smashing, they employ revolting methods, they lack moral scruples, they break the law. Nevertheless, since they are merely hired agents, it is correct to say that the detective agencies are not the real force opposed to the workers. Facing the workers in their struggle for unionization and collective bargaining are the industrialists who hire the agencies to carry on their work of destruction and pay them handsomely for it.

The workers' struggle for unionization is a hard one. The employing class is a formidable enemy. Then why do workers persist in the fight? Chief Justice Hughes of the United States Supreme Court gave the answer in the majority decision in the Jones-Laughlin Labor Board Case: "Long ago we stated the reason for labor organizations. We said that they were organized out of the necessities of the situation; that a single employee was helpless in dealing with an employer; that he was dependent ordinarily on his daily wage for the maintenance of himself and family; that if the employer refused to pay him the wages that he thought fair, he was nevertheless unable to leave the employ and resist arbitrary and unfair treatment; that union was essential to give laborers opportunity to deal on an equality with their employer."

This is not the first time that the United States Supreme Court has held that workers standing alone are not on equal terms with employers, that only by organizing into unions can they expect to "deal on an equality with their employer." As long ago as 1898 the Court held that "the proprietors of these establishments and their operatives [workers] do not stand upon an equality . . . the proprietors lay down the rules and the laborers are practically constrained to obey them."

One group wants to sell labor, the other group wants to buy labor. But according to the Supreme Court and to every student of the subject, the two groups are not equal in strength. The laborers organize into unions so they can have a voice, with the proprietors, in "laying down the rules." That's the purpose of unionization, of collective bargaining. The men who join labor unions are the workers who have learned from experience, and from the Supreme Court and other official government bodies, that only in union can they obtain the strength they need to bargain on equal terms with their employers.

Any one reading the sugared statements of our captains of industry would never for a moment believe that they are opposed to this fundamental first step of their workers. No dispute between capital and labor is ever complete without a pretty speech by the employer that he is not at all opposed to unionization or collective bargaining. That's what he says. What he does is quite another matter. This is an old story. It was true many years ago. It was true in 1912. It is true today.

The 1912 experience is illuminating. In that year Congress passed an act calling for the creation of a Commission on Industrial Relations, which was to inquire into the existing relations between employers and employees. The Commission consisted of nine members, three representing the employers, three the employees, and three the general public. The Commission held public hearings for about six months; it heard witnesses affiliated with employers, with labor, and with neither. Part of its report reads: "It is very significant that out of 230 representatives of the interests of employers, chosen largely on the recommendations of their own organizations, less than half a dozen have denied the propriety of collective action on the part of employees. *A considerable number of these witnesses have, however, testified that they denied in practice what they admitted to be right in theory."*

This denial of the workers' right to organize still goes on. It is the primary cause of labor disputes. Contrary to general opinion, the fact is that in most of the strikes that are called in the U. S., *the major issue is not wages and hours,* but matters pertaining *to union organization and recognition.* The latest figures from the U. S. Department of Labor show that this is true:

MAJOR ISSUES INVOLVED IN STRIKES, 1934–1936

All issues	1934		1935		1936	
	Number	Per cent of total	Number	Per cent	Number	Per cent
	1856	100.0	2014	100.0	2156	100.0
Wages and hours......	727	39.3	769	38.2	756	35.1
Union organization....	853	45.9	952	47.3	1083	50.2
Miscellaneous........	276	14.8	293	14.5	317	14.7

Notice that in every case, the issue of union organization and recognition was the primary cause of strikes; and that in 1936, this was the issue involved in more than half the disputes.

The blame for much of our industrial warfare thus lies at the doorstep of those employers who refuse to allow workers to unionize and have representatives of their own choosing. In the Jones-Laughlin decision the Supreme Court said this in so many words: "Experience has abundantly demonstrated that the recognition of the right of employees to self-organization and to have representatives of their own choosing for the purpose of collective bargaining is often an essential condition of industrial peace. *Refusal to confer and negotiate has been one of the most prolific causes of strife.* This is such an outstanding fact in the history of labor disturbances that it is a proper subject of judicial notice and requires no citation of instances."

There was a time when employers were within their legal rights in refusing "to confer and negotiate." But today that is no longer true. The fact that some industrialists still continue to defy the law, places squarely on their shoulders the responsibility for the bloodshed resulting from industrial strife. It is a discouraging fact that so many of them — leaders in their communities — continue to carry that responsibility. They are quick to shout "agitators" as soon as a strike breaks out, yet it is they who are the real agitators, they who are the true disturbers of the peace.

When *The New York Herald Tribune* in its lead editorial on February 10, 1937 said, "It is now recognized by custom and law in this country that labor has the right to organize, to bargain collectively through representatives of its own choosing and to strike", it was only half correct. *It is now recognized by law* — the National Labor Relations Act, passed by Congress in July 1935, gave labor those rights. *But it is not now recognized by custom* — no employer of labor spies recognizes it. The policies of Congress as declared in the Wagner Act are completely defeated by industrial espionage. Those industrialists who have hired labor spies have violated the law.

What are we to think of these revelations of unfair and illegal industrial practices on the part of employers? Mr. Walter Lippmann, in his column in *The Herald Tribune*, March 6, 1937, tells us what to think: "As long as big business stood intrenched behind its Pinkertons and its dogmas, it was in fact imbued with the psychology of class war, however much it might deplore the idea when openly preached from a soapbox. The refusal to recognize the unions and to negotiate with them could not by any possibility be described as an attitude of peace; among nations the equivalent is a refusal to have diplomatic relations, an act just short of war which generally leads to war."

Thus put on our guard by Mr. Lippmann we need not be taken in by such statements as the following made by Mr. Alfred P. Sloan, Jr. on July 26, 1934: "The Management of General Motors holds that there is no real conflict of interests between employers and employees . . . Enlightened employers and enlightened employees realize that they have a mutuality of interests such as to dictate the wisdom of maintaining the highest degree of cooperation and harmonious relations."

We have learned that these are merely words without substance. Behind them is the reality of the class war, as exemplified in the use of Pinkerton spies.

Similarly, when the sit-down strikers are in possession of the Chrysler plant, and Mr. K. T. Keller, president of the Chrysler Corporation, runs a full-page statement in the newspapers of the country in which the following assertion is made: "This company has conducted its industrial relations by and in accordance with general acknowledged standards of fairness and equity" — we are not surprised. We are now aware that sugarcoated sweet phrases covering the bitter pill of class war have long been prescribed for labor by capital. We leave to others the impossible task of reconciling the employment of Corporations Auxiliary spies with "standards of fairness and equity."

Occasionally by accident, we are given the unusual opportunity to get behind the scenes as one of the employing class talks to another. Then the difference between their silken phrases offered for public consumption and their real attitude becomes clear. A letter to Commissioner Sayre of the N.M.T.A. throws some light on the private thinking of these representatives of the powerful metal trades manufacturers:

COLUMBUS BRANCH N.M.T.A.
July 7, 1936

Dear Homer:
   . . . What do you think of the advisability of having an operative whose business it would be to circulate generally and

keep us informed in regard to the activities of *our friend the enemy?* . . .

H. L. ENNIS,
Secretary.

SENATOR LA FOLLETTE. What is your interpretation, Mr. Sayre, of the phrase "the activities of our friend the enemy" in this letter?

MR. SAYRE. Well, I assume that Mr. Ennis refers to the activities of the labor organizations which are attempting to unionize the plants of the members of the association . . .

There we have it. The "enemy" is the labor organizations which attempt to unionize. That the law gives these organizations that right is for the N.M.T.A. beside the point.

That's frankness in private. Frankness in the open is indeed rare; so we are deeply indebted to Mr. Hal Smith, counsel of the Michigan Manufacturers' Association, who seems to express the real point of view of the employers' group. "We know of no reason why an employer in his plant should not have the right to employ a detective. We see no reflection in any way in the employment of detectives. 'Detective' and 'spy' are two names that are used in a derogatory sense, but *even a spy has a necessary place in time of war,* and it is not always that they are to be condemned."

This spokesman for the manufacturers leaves us no choice. We realize, from his statement, that Mr. Lippmann and the "soapbox preachers" are right — employers believe in and wage class war.

It is waged in a number of ways. Spying is only one weapon in the class war. When that fails, when the unions continue to enroll members in spite of the work of stool-pigeons, then open violence is tried.

The Ford Motor Company recently provided a perfect illustration. There was, as always, the usual statement that the men may join the union if they so desire:

Ford Says His Men
May "Join Anything"

They Are "Free," He Declares, but Would Be "Foolish" to Sign Up in Labor Union

DETROIT, April 13 (AP).—Henry Ford declared today that his employees were "free to join anything they want to."

"They have always been free to join any church, any lodge or any union they want to," he said in his first interview after the Supreme Court decision upholding the Wagner Labor Relations Act.

"Of course I think they are foolish if they join any union. They will lose their liberty and all they will get is the right of paying dues to somebody."

Mr. Ford here makes the flat assertion that his men "have always been free to join any union they want to." That statement is simply not true. Ford employees have never been free to join a union. The spy system in the Ford plant has long been notorious. The Ford Company does not hire detective agencies — it has its own elaborate spy system under the direction of Mr. Harry H. Bennett. (In this respect it is not alone — many companies have their own service.) The complete story of how Mr. Bennett's "service men" operate has never been told, but enough is known to give the lie to Henry Ford's statement. In December, 1934, before the President's joint NRA-Labor Department inquiry, the testimony of the attorney for the Mechanics' Educational Society of America was taken. Here is *The New York Times* account of that testimony: "Mr. Sugar said that the Ford Motor Company's 'service' men were in the habit of looking through the employes' lunch boxes and clothes in the lockers to find evidence of trade union literature.

"According to Mr. Sugar, motion pictures were made of a demonstration of automobile employes by the Ford Company, the films were developed and examined and those found to have been Ford workers were discharged. He promised to furnish the commission with the names of those discharged."

How can Mr. Ford's and Mr. Sugar's statements be reconciled? They cannot. One of them is trying to pull a fast one. Which one? Up until May 26, 1937, either case might have been hard to prove definitely. But on that day sbmething happened which makes it easy to judge.

The United Automobile Workers, having signed agreements with both General Motors and the Chrysler Corporation, next turned their attention to the Ford Motor Company. The union organizers asked for and received permission from the Dearborn City Council to distribute union leaflets to Ford workers on May 26. Now look at the pictures (facing page 106) for what happened. (Also see Frankensteen's own account, Appendix F.)

The captions are taken from *The New York World-Telegram* of May 27. Evidently the editor of this paper did not believe Harry Bennett's explanation of who did the slugging. Here is Bennett's statement: "The affair was deliberately provoked by union officials . . . I know definitely no Ford service men or plant police were involved in any way in the fight. As a matter of fact, the service men had issued instructions the union people could come and distribute their pamphlets at the gate so long as they didn't interfere with employes at work.

"The union men were beaten by regular Ford employes who were on their way to work on the afternoon shift . . ."

The World-Telegram caption writer was not taken in by Bennett's statement. He didn't believe that the sluggers were "regular Ford employes." He labels them what they were: "Ford's service men." Look at the next picture and you can make your own guess. See the handcuffs sticking out of the back pocket of the "worker" at the left? Ever hear of an auto worker who needed handcuffs on his job? The camera doesn't lie. The service men know that — which explains why "the only victims of the fighting besides the unionists were several of the photographers at the scene."

Violence. Union organizers suddenly beaten, kicked, and driven away. That is the Ford Motor Company's law-breaking answer to the U.A.W.A.'s attempt to unionize Ford workers. (IRONICAL NOTE: On page 3 of *The New York Times* of May 27, 1937, just below the picture showing the beating of Frankensteen, is a story whose headline reads: "Ford Assets Rose to $717,359,366 in 1936; Profit and Loss Account Gained $19,689,021.")

Four days after the beating at Ford's, on May 30, in Chicago, more violence. Another manifestation of the class war. Ten killed, forty injured. Why? Because the Republic Steel Company, continuing its traditional anti-union policy, chose not to sign an agreement with the Steel Workers Organizing Committee of the C.I.O. A strike resulted. On Memorial Day, about a thousand union sympathizers, including many women and children, marched in peaceful fashion toward the Republic Steel Company plant. They were unarmed. They were several blocks from the gate of the plant, *not even on company grounds*, when the Chicago police in their capacity as "protectors of the company's property," fired, threw tear gas bombs, then attacked with clubs. The death list is evidence of where the responsibility for the slaughter lies. *Not a single policeman was shot.*

Joseph Hickey, one of the wounded, tells what happened: "I went to the meeting and they decided to make a picket line at the front of the company. I went out with the rest of them and started to walk over to the plant. I was about 100 yards behind the head of the line when the uproar began. They were like trapped rats, panic-stricken, terrified.

"I saw a woman fall as she was being clubbed by the policemen. She was bleeding and looked like she was dying. I ran over to help her and leaned down to pick her up, when the police hit me over the head. I was out after that."

So horrible was the massacre that Paramount News, which filmed the entire episode, found it advisable not to release the film for public showings. The editor explained his action with these words: "Our pictures depict a tense and nerve-wracking episode, which, in certain sections of the country, might very well incite local riot and perhaps riotous demonstrations in theaters, leading to further casualties." This news editor was not faint-hearted. He knew his picture. So brutal a slaughter of innocent men, women, and children has seldom before occurred in the United States — and the film shows it clearly. Read, in Appendix G, the story the suppressed film tells, written by a person who saw it.

Workers beaten, sent to the hospital, killed. This is the price of the Republic Steel Company's refusal to sign a contract with the union. The Carnegie-Illinois Steel Company has signed such a contract — and there is peace. The Jones and Laughlin Steel Corporation agreed to an election under the supervision of the N.L.R.B.; the employees voted 17,412 for the C.I.O. union, 7,207 against; Jones-Laughlin signed with the union — and there is peace. Over 130 steel companies have signed contracts with the union — and there is peace. But Republic Steel refuses to sign — and blood is spilled.

The violence in this case was police violence. That often happens as a result of industrialists' unwillingness to deal with unions. And direct violence on the part of thugs hired by the employers also happens often. The horrible condition of affairs in Harlan County, Kentucky, which has given that place the well-deserved name of "Bloody Harlan," is known to all. Union meetings broken up by riflemen; the murder of the son of a preacher who was a union organizer; the frequent beatings of union organizers; the dynamiting of their cars and hotel rooms; the incarceration of union members in an iron cage under a porch belonging to a coal firm; Harlan "justice" as portrayed by the judge who phoned a coal operator to ask him how to dispose of the case of an arrested union organizer — all this and more has been disclosed by the La Follette committee. But we have learned to expect anything to happen in the feudal domain which is Bloody Harlan.   It's almost as if Harlan County were not a part of the United States. But it is — and it has its counterpart in other sections.

In 1936 the employees of the Pekin Distilling Company in Pekin, Illinois, complained to the Labor Relations Board of espionage in the plant. The Board's investigation was hamstrung at every turn by court action on the part of the company. The men went out on strike. The situation was tense. This was the moment chosen by the Peoria Manufacturers' Association to deputize two gunmen with criminal records, as strike-breakers. One of the thugs, Charles Summers, was questioned by the state superintendent of supervision of parolees. Here is the testimony from the record:

> *Question:* Were you ever requested, or was the suggestion made to you, or were you ordered, to bump off, knock off, get rid of, or put in the hospital, a fellow by the name of Kinsella and a fellow by the name of Wilkie?
>
> *Answer:* Yes. Not Wilkie, but Kinsella.
>
> *Q.* Charlie, will you give the details in reference to the best of your recollection?
>
> *A.* Well, in short, this Kinsella was causing a lot of trouble for the Manufacturers' Association, and Mr. Roark [secretary of the Association] *thought it would be a good idea to put him in the hospital* for a while. He offered me $50, $25 of which he advanced. That's all there was to it . . .

The scene shifts from Illinois to Alabama. Mr. Blaine Owen is active in union work there. Mr. Le May, assistant to the president of the Tennessee Coal Iron and Railroad Company, doesn't like unions. A Pinkerton solicitor tries to get some business from him. Here is part of the letter the Pink wrote to Littlejohn of the Atlanta office: "On my last two trips through Birmingham I have called upon Mr. E. D. Le May, assistant to the President of the Tennessee Coal and Iron Railroad . . . Mr. Le May confidently told me that in the case of one very active Communist, Blaine Owens, *they pri-*

*vately had him taken on a week's 'fishing trip' and worked on him sev-
eral times a day during that period,* with the result that he left Birmingham permanently."

Understand, these quotations are not from the diary of a master
racketeer. These orders to "put him in the hospital," and "work on
him," are issued by respectable employers. What it means to be a
union organizer in conflict with the T. C. & I., what it means to be
taken on a "fishing trip," has been described by Blaine Owen. Read
his account in Appendix H.

Sometimes getting rid of a troublesome union man is the company's idea, occasionally it springs from the spy. One N.M.T.A.
operative's report contains the significant words, "If Newbold and
one or two others could be eliminated, there would be no trouble."
A Pinkerton spy reports, "I believe if Shaw, Baum, and Scholle
were eliminated and the company talked to the people that main-
tain the picket line, an agreement could be reached." Remember,
again, these reports are sent, not to a Dutch Schultz or an Al
Capone, but to the heads of big manufacturing firms.

Such reports would not be sent if those industrialists were not in a
mood to receive them. Unfortunately they are. The beatings and
killings of active union men do not come as a surprise to them.
Where these industrialists do not themselves engineer the beatings,
they are at least aware that they are going to happen. Clifton Slusser, vice-president and factory manager of Goodyear Tire and
Rubber Co., is on the stand, talking about the Gadsden, Alabama
plant of Goodyear:

SENATOR LA FOLLETTE. Do you recall that . . . you offered
to bet Mr. Pollard or Mr. Ricketts $100 that no union man
could organize the employees in the Gadsden plant of Goodyear?

MR. SLUSSER. I do not recall having made him an offer of a
bet, but I did make the statement that they could not go to
Gadsden, in my opinion, or go south of the Mason-Dixon line

and do and say these things that they were doing and saying in Akron.

. . .

SENATOR LA FOLLETTE. Do you recall stating words to this ef-fect, that if an organizer did get off the train he would have to come back on a stretcher?

MR. SLUSSER. No; I told him he might get his head knocked off. (Laughter)

Mr. Sherman H. Dalrymple, union organizer who attempted to address a meeting of Goodyear employees in Gadsden, Alabama, followed Mr. Slusser on the witness stand. His testimony that the meeting was broken up by Goodyear's "flying squadron," and that "his head was knocked off" to the extent that he was sent to the hospital suffering from concussion of the brain, proved how great a prophet Slusser was.

Mr. C. D. Lesley, a Goodyear employee for nine years, testified that the "flying squadron" was given military training for a period of one month. Read his testimony. The Goodyear Co. anticipated that a strike might develop. A strike for this great company meant a war, nothing less:

SENATOR LA FOLLETTE. How often did the men go to the hall for this training?

MR. LESLEY. Oh, 3 to 4 days a week, depending on just how serious they thought this thing was that they expected to develop.

SENATOR LA FOLLETTE. And how long did the training period last?

MR. LESLEY. I think I am safe in saying close to a month.

SENATOR LA FOLLETTE. And each one of these sessions of drill that you had, how long would they last on the average?

MR. LESLEY. About two hours.

. . .

SENATOR LA FOLLETTE. Did you receive any training as to the use of any kind of weapons, gas weapons or others?

MR. LESLEY. There were general instructions given to the entire group in the use of a gas gun and the position of a man using this gun in the various formations.

. . .

SENATOR LA FOLLETTE. What sort of particular formations did you practice that had to do with riots?

MR. LESLEY. Well, the one that they stuck to very close was what is known as the wedge formation.

. . .

SENATOR LA FOLLETTE. Describe that.

MR. LESLEY. Well, the formation is made by a group of men, and when they are in their position the formation, or it appears as though it is a wedge with a spearpoint and so forth, and the leading man is supposed to be the man to lead into the group, and the others are to protect him. The position of this gas man is in the center, and it is for his protection presumably.

SENATOR LA FOLLETTE. Would you describe this as an offensive or defensive formation?

MR. LESLEY. Offensive; absolutely.

Keep that "offensive formation" in mind next time you read about company guards killing picketers, "in defense of company property."

Mr. Lesley was not telling a fairy tale. This military training of Goodyear workers happened. It happened at the other rubber plants too. One of the experts in charge, Joseph J. Johnston, Colonel of Cavalry of the Ohio National Guard Reserve, had done a good job. He felt that in applying for a similar position with other firms he could give the Akron rubber companies as reference. He writes to Mr. C. E. Mitchell, Industrial Relations Department, General Motors Corporation, Detroit, Michigan:

My Dear Sir: During the threatened labor trouble in the rubber industry in Akron, I was employed by the Akron rubber companies to organize and train the plant protection units and take general charge of plant defense. By getting to work well in advance of the threatened trouble, I believe we were able to prevent the strike. *I had fully equipped and trained 1500 men.*

I am writing to you to inquire if you would be in need of service along this line. I can refer you to Mr. Herbert Cook in charge of factory safety and defense, the B. F. Goodrich Company, Akron, and Mr. William Reese of the same capacity at the Firestone Rubber Company, Akron, or any of the officials of these companies that you would care to write to. I might also refer you to Sheriff James Flower of Summit County, Akron, whose force I assisted in training.

Now we don't know whether or not Colonel Johnston got the job with General Motors. But we do know that if he did get it, and if he was sent to Flint to train Chevrolet or Buick workers, he found all the equipment he needed waiting for him. P. H. Kilean, Lake Erie Chemical Company agent, wrote to Mr. Ailes on September 30, 1933:

Ship to James V. Mills, chief of police, city of Flint, Michigan the following: Ten no. 16 gun clubs and ten dozen (120) no. 16-A shells for same . . . Do not bill the city of Flint for this material. Instead send the bill to the Manufacturers Association of Flint, 901 Industrial Bank Building. Mail it for the attention of James Farber, manager. Mr. Farber is the one who telephoned me this order this morning.

For your own information only, *I have reason to believe this material is for the Chevrolet Motor Company;* but they do not want it advertised or generally known that they are the buyers.

Several months later, Mr. Kilean comes through again with an order, this time for Buick. Same secrecy to be observed:

Dear Mr. Ailes: For your records, please be advised that I sold to the Buick Motor Company, Flint, Michigan, two long

range gas guns, single action, of the hammer-hinged type, at
$40 each, and 12 long range tear gas charges for these guns, at
$90 a dozen, or a total of $170.

The Buick wanted this material delivered personally to their
plant protection department, to circumvent the receiving department, so I took it up myself Wednesday.

Now all this is particularly interesting in the light of a request for
tear gas made to Lake Erie by the other side in the class war. What
happens if a union wants to arm itself in a manner similar to that of
Chevrolet, Buick, and other industrial firms? Will the Lake Erie,
like the armament industry, sell to both sides? It will not. The class
war is evidently different from ordinary wars. Witness this letter
dated May 13, 1936, from Mr. Ailes to the International Brotherhood, Chauffeurs and Helpers of Bridgeport, Connecticut:

> Gentlemen: *We are restricting the sale of our tear gas weapons
> to law-enforcement agencies,* and therefore are not in a position
> to quote, in answer to your letter of May 10th. We do not sell
> through dealers . . .
>
> THE LAKE ERIE CHEMICAL COMPANY
> A. S. Ailes, Vice President

That Mr. Ailes was not telling the truth in the italicized sentence
above, you have already seen from the sale to Chevrolet and Buick.
On the stand, he testified that thirty to thirty-five percent of Lake
Erie's sales went to individuals or corporations; Mr. Engelhart, sales
manager of the Manville Manufacturing Co., testified that fifty
percent of his company's sales were industrial.

The map below, drawn by the La Follette committee, shows that
preparing for violent industrial war is not restricted to a few plants
— it seems to be part of the pattern of American industry, like
spying.

Industrialists love to make speeches about "The American
Way." Billboards all over our country are plastered with those

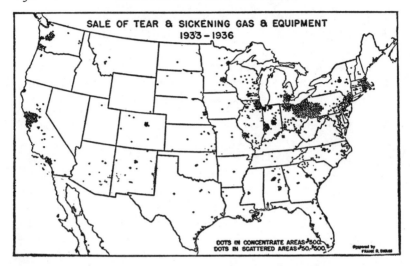

SALE OF TEAR & SICKENING GAS & EQUIPMENT
1933 – 1936

DOTS IN CONCENTRATE AREAS – 500
DOTS IN SCATTERED AREAS – 50 – 500

familiar words — "The American Way." In Europe there is also a class war. Yet a map like the one above, before the advent of the Nazis, could not have been understood by a European. And labor spying by hired detective agencies is also unknown there. It is completely an American phenomenon. Is this what our industrialists mean by "The American Way"?

VIII. What Is To Be Done?

THE MAJOR PURPOSE of industrial espionage is union-prevention and union-smashing. This is a violation of the laws of our country. Spying defeats the policy of Congress, declared in the Wagner Act, that labor should have the right to organize.

What is to be done?

Employers who want to obey the law will know what to do. They must give up the practice of hiring spy agencies. This does not mean that they are to replace hired spies with their own plant spies. No. They must not interfere in any way with the efforts of their employees to organize, to join unions.

Employees should do immediately what the law gives them a right to do — organize. They should join trade unions. It is all to the good that the Wagner Act is on the statute books; that Wisconsin and Indiana have laws requiring the registration of operatives. Workers should demand the enforcement of these laws and the passage of other laws against the use of spy agencies. Yet that is not enough. Workers must not rely on legislation alone to make it impossible for law-breaking employers to deprive them of their rights. The way to win for all time the right to join trade unions is to exercise that right, now. Legislation helps, but without the organized might of the united workers behind them, law makers can do very little. The only way for workers to advance their own interests is by building up and strengthening their own organization — the trade union.

But how is that possible so long as employers continue to plant spies in unions to disrupt worker organization? It is possible. It can be done. Unions can be organized in spite of crooked spy activities. They have been. They will be.

However, the job of union-building is not easy. It must be approached seriously and sensibly, with determination to succeed. If workers tackle the job in that spirit, the outlook will not be discouraging. Unions have discovered and exposed spies before. They can do it again.

The essential first step is for every worker to make it his task to build the union, just as the spy makes it his task to tear it down. This means that every union member must be an active union member, interested in what is going on, and doing his share of the work. Where there is trade union democracy, where all members are alive to what is happening, where they analyze the problems, discuss the solutions, and participate in the decisions, there the spy cannot so easily do his deadly work. Where there is trade union bureaucracy, where union affairs are given over to a handful of officers, where it is left to a small group to run the show, there the spy's job of ruining the show is that much simpler.

Every union member must adopt the spy's tactic of keeping his eyes and ears open. He must try to understand what is happening in his organization and be on the alert for sabotage. Are committee members doing the work they are supposed to do? Was that Red-baiting speech a cover for inactivity or treachery on the part of the member who delivered it? The member who always goes in for hair-splitting — is he really honest, or is he a wrecker? These are only a few of the things to be observed. But they must be observed calmly and carefully. The fact that stool-pigeons are planted in trade unions is no reason for undue suspicion, or for going off half-cocked on a wild spy-hunt. Union members must be absolutely certain of their case before they accuse a fellow member of being a spy.

Just as it is important for every union member to keep his eyes and ears open, so it is important for him to keep his mouth shut. He must not talk too much — particularly to the fellow who asks too much. The danger of "shooting off your mouth" is real. Witness the case of Charles Jennings, a union organizer who should have known better. A spy for the N.M.T.A. writes to Mr. Stringham: "In a little talk with Mr. Earl I told him I had made a close contact with one Charles Jennings, of Jersey City. Jennings is the State or general organizer for the A. F. of L. *He tells me quite freely of his movements and plans regarding organization work.* Of course he does not suspect my motives."

Obviously such behavior on the part of a union man is downright stupidity. Spies can be licked — but an important first requirement is the exercise of good common sense by union members.

Despite the fact that the Wagner Act has outlawed the employment of undercover operatives to forestall unionization, despite the fact that the Supreme Court has upheld that Act, some employers will continue to use spies. They will continue to use them because they believe that spies are necessary in the conduct of business today. The fact that this is not true doesn't help the situation any. So long as employers believe it is true, spies will be hired. When Mr. O. P. Briggs was Commissioner of the National Founders' Association, he said that the spy system was absolutely essential: "I regard this as one of the very best investments the Association makes. Without it, I would hardly know how to direct the work of the Association. It seems to be an indispensable requisite to good results."

When Mr. Weckler was on the stand, he indicated that he too thought there was some excuse for the spy system. In answer to a question from Senator Thomas, he said, "I think it is very essential that an employer know the situations which surround his business. This is one method of getting information."

Over twenty years ago, General Atterbury of the Pennsylvania Railroad, testifying before the Industrial Relations Commission, put the matter bluntly: "We have a spy system. There will always be one until a better method of handling labor relations is developed."

Employers should realize that "a better method of handling labor relations" has been developed. It is for them to grant to labor its fundamental right to organize and to bargain collectively through representatives of its own choosing. That is the "better method" which makes the spy system unnecessary.

Fair-minded employers will realize that in granting that right to labor, they are granting only what they have always enjoyed themselves. In the words of the Supreme Court, "Employes have as clear a right to organize and select their representatives for lawful purposes as the respondent [employer] has to organize its business and select its own officers and agents."

This means, of course, that industry must be prepared to give up its outworn slogan that has caused so much trouble, "Nobody is going to tell me how to run my business." That must be given up because it no longer holds. In the twentieth century it is not accurate to speak of a business as "my business." Today, business is the affair of both the employer and the employee. Fixing the conditions of work, the hours and the wages, is the business of *both* the boss and the worker. It is not possible, today, to permit a single employer, or a group of employers, to determine the conditions of labor; *labor's representatives must have an equal voice in the determination of those conditions.* This participation by those who work in the decisions affecting their livelihood is nothing more or less than democracy in industry. It is as important as democracy in politics if not more so.

Labor's voice, when it is heard, must not be that of individuals shouting each other down. It must be a collective voice. Only through genuine collective bargaining can labor attain the equality with capital that is its right. The Wagner Act states specifically that: "Representatives designated or selected for the purposes of collective bargaining by the majority of the employees in a unit appropriate for such purposes, shall be the exclusive representatives *of all the employees* in such unit for the purposes of collective bargaining in respect to rates of pay, wages, hours of employment, or other conditions of employment."

This does not mean that individual employees or groups may not present their grievances to the employer. Not at all. It does mean, however, that they are prevented from making separate agreements with the employer in regard to hours, wages, and working conditions, which are the sole function of the bargaining agency.

This, again, is the democratic method. Those anti-union employers who have suddenly become concerned with the rights of the minority (strangely enough, they never gave a thought to this before the passage of the Wagner Act) are guilty of distortion of the facts. Industry is run on the principle of majority rule; so is politics. Many millions of Americans voted for Landon in the last election; many more millions voted for Roosevelt. Roosevelt is the president not alone of those people who voted for him, but of all the people.

To argue against collective bargaining on the further ground that it is not necessary, because employers have always been willing to listen to the grievances of their employees, is contrary to the spirit of democracy. The Commission on Industrial Relations pointed this out in a striking passage: "A great deal of testimony has been introduced to show that the employers who refuse to deal collectively with their workmen do in fact grant audiences at which the grievances of their workmen may be presented. One is repelled rather than impressed by the insistence with which this idea has been presented. Every tyrant in history has on stated days granted audiences to which his faithful subjects might bring their complaints against his officers and agents. At these audiences, in theory at least, even the poorest widow might be heard by her sovereign in her search for justice. That justice was never secured under such conditions, except at the whim of the tyrant is sure. It is equally sure that in industry justice can never be attained by such a method."

Some die-hard employers who see that collective bargaining has come to stay have resorted to two tricks to retain their dictatorial power: the first is to grant collective bargaining — to a company union; the second is to build up the myth that all union leaders are crooks or Reds. Intelligent workers will not be fooled by either manoeuvre.

The company union is a fake. It is a dummy organization which enables the employer to control both sides of the table when there is any attempt at collective bargaining. Workers' representatives in a company union cannot be free and fearless, because they are paid their wages by the man with whom they are negotiating. The company union, by its nature, prevents the workers in one plant from organizing with workers in other plants. Senator Robinson on April 7, 1937, hit the nail on the head in a speech delivered on the floor of the Senate: "Whenever an organization is fostered and promoted and financed by the company itself for the purpose of controlling the laborers and preventing them from exercising the rights which sound public policy guarantees to them it constitutes a 'company union.' Of course, such union is not always heralded as a scheme or enterprise to interfere with the rights of laborers, but, as a matter of fact, the object is to control the workers themselves, particularly in their exercise of the right of collective bargaining."

Workers must steer clear of company unions, employees' associations, and the like. They must profit from the example of the employers — organize in groups of their own for their own interests.

They must not let themselves be fooled by the lies about trade unions, spread by the splitters of the ranks of labor. The leaders of the trade unions are not crooks — in most unions there is a very strict periodic accounting of all union funds. The instances of union officers running off with the money are few — and often the crook is a spy sent in to rob the treasury. Racketeering by union leaders does occur, but it is highly exaggerated. There is less racketeering by union leaders than by business leaders. Trade union dues are low when thought of in terms of the benefits received. Company union dues, where they exist at all, are lower — they should be because the benefits go to the employer, not to the worker. The leaders and members of trade unions are not "Reds"; they are Democrats, Republicans, Socialists, Communists, Catholics, Jews, Protestants, just as in the business world.

What is to be done?

How can the despicable spy system be destroyed? Here is the answer, given by John L. Lewis, after the U.A.W.A. had signed a contract with General Motors: "There will now be no need for labor spies, for obviously everybody will know who the union members are. They have no secrets and the union will be willing to advise General Motors of any action taken at meetings. The same situation will now prevail as obtains in the mining industry, where there are no secrets and where detective agencies are starving to death. This detective thing is a ghastly chapter in the history of General Motors and the whole industry."

Many years ago, Henry Demarest Lloyd, a great American, made a profound observation about the ghastly business of industrial espionage. He said, "A spy at one end of an institution proves that there is a tyrant at the other."

In the United States of America there is no room for tyrants. To get rid of the tyranny in American industry is the job of the workers of America. There is only one way to do it —

ORGANIZE!

APPENDIX

A.

LIST OF DETECTIVE AGENCIES
AS OF APRIL 1936

[NOTE. — This list is based.on that contained in Cabot Fund Report, as of 1920; agencies added are preceded by an asterisk (*).]

Abbott's Inc., Chicago.
*Acme Detective Agency, San Francisco, Calif.
*Active Industrial Service, New York City.
Addis Detective Agency, Philadelphia.
A. D. T. Protective Service, Cincinnati.
*Aetna Judicial Service, New York.
*A. A. Ahner Detective Agency, St. Louis, Mo. (*See* Industrial Investigators and Engineers, Inc.)
Alexander & Leweck, Milwaukee.
*American Confidential Bureau (Charles W. Hansen), New York City, 605 Fifth Avenue.
American Detective Service Co., Chicago.
*American Loyalty League, San Francisco, Calif.
*American Plan, George W. Frothingham, president, and John A. Lucett, secretary, Cleveland, Ohio.
*American Vigilant Intelligence Federation, H. A. Jung, Chicago.
Armsworth & Cavett Agency, Pittsburgh.
Ascher Detective Agency, New York City.
*Aster Detective Service (William M. Tivoli), New York City.
*Atlas Detective Bureau, Philadelphia, Pa.

Baldwin-Felts Agency, Roanoke, Va.; Bluefields, W. Va.
*Bargron Detective Agency, Rockford, Ill.
*Barthell Detective Agency, Nashville, Tenn.
*Bell Detective Service, Philadelphia, Pa.
Bergoff Bros., New York City. (Bergoff Industrial Service, Inc., 551 Fifth Avenue, New York.)
*Berkshire Detective Agency, Brooklyn, N. Y. (Joe Lawrence, alias Joseph La Bataglia).
*Bernhard Haas, New York City.
B & M Secret Service Bureau, Detroit.
*Bodeker National Detective Agency, Birmingham, Ala., and in Chattanooga.
*H. S. Boulin, New York City.
*Bowers Detective Service, Philadelphia, Pa.
*R. W. Bridgman Detective Bureau. (*See* Morse Detective and Patrol Service.)
*S. S. Brody, Buffalo, N. Y.
P. J. Burke National Detective Agency, Boston.
Burr-Herr Agency, Chicago.
Burton Detective Agency, Cleveland.
Walter J. Burns, Detroit, Mich.
William J. Burns, International Detective Agency, Inc., New York City. Branch offices in other cities. Representing American Bankers' Association. Criminal, general, industrial, and commercial detective work. Branch offices at Atlanta, Baltimore, Birmingham, Boston, Brussels, Bridgeport, Buffalo, Chicago, Cincinnati, Cleveland, Dallas, Denver,

Des Moines, Detroit, El Paso, Houston, Jacksonville, Kansas City, London, Los Angeles, Memphis, Miami, Minneapolis, Montreal, New Orleans, New York, Oklahoma City, Paris, Philadelphia, Pittsburgh, Portland, Providence, Richmond, Salt Lake City, San Francisco, Seattle, Spokane, St. Louis, St. Paul, Toronto, Vancouver, Washington, D. C., Wilkes-Barre.

Butler System of Industrial Surveys, New York.

H. J. Carling, St. Paul.

*Central Industrial Service (see R. A. and I. Co.), Pittsburgh, Pa.

*Clarke's Detective Agency, Buffalo, N. Y.

R. J. Coach Co., Cleveland.

*Harry J. Connors (aided by James Walsh), New York.

*Contra Costa County Industrial Association, Richmond, Calif.

*Thomas J. Corbally Detective Agency, Inc., Newark, N. J.

Corporations Auxiliary Co., New York City, incorporated in Ohio, uses name "International Auxiliary Co." in New York State. Employment service under name of "Eastern Contracting & Engineering Co." at same address. Other offices at Chicago, Cleveland, St. Louis, Buffalo, Milwaukee, Pittsburgh, Cincinnati, and Detroit.

Corporations Service Bureau, Detroit.

*Corporations Service Investigation Corporation, Youngstown, Ohio. (See National Corporations Service, Inc.)

*D. F. Costello Bureau, San Francisco, Calif.

Cal Crim Agency, Cincinnati.

*Cresswell Agency, Akron Savings & Loan Building, Akron, Ohio.

*H. C. Cumming Detective Agency, Reading, Pa.

*Russell Davis, San Francisco, Calif.

*W. C. Dannenberg, 111 West Monroe Street, Chicago.

*Dawn Patrol, Detroit, Mich.

*Dougherty's Detective Bureau, New York City.

*W. Howard Downey and Associates, New York, Chicago, Atlanta, Toronto.

*Drummond Detective Agency, 521 Fifth Avenue, New York.

Dunn's National Detective Agency, Detroit.

*Arthur F. Eagan, New York City.

*Eagle and Industrial Associates, New York City. (See Eagle Detective Agency; Sherwood Detective Bureau.)

Eagle Detective Agency, New York City. (See Sherwood Detective Bureau; Eagle Industrial Associates.)

*Eastern Engineering Co.

Employer's Detective Service, St. Paul.

Farley Detective and Strikebreaking Agency, Chicago, Ill., Milwaukee. Principal, Jim Farley, dean of American strikebreakers.

*Farrah Secret Service, Detroit, Mich.

John E. Ferris Intelligence Service, Milwaukee.

*Fred Fields Detective Agency, Cleveland.

*William J. Flynn Agency, New York City, 1457 Broadway.

*Forbes International Detective Agency, Philadelphia, Pa.

Robert J. Foster Service, New York City.

*Franklin & Stoner, New York City, Philadelphia.

Gale National Detective Agency, St. Paul.

*Gignat Secret Service, Private Detective Agency, San Francisco, Calif.

Gordon & Allen, St. Paul.

F. P. Gordon Detective Bureau, Milwaukee.

Goldsmith Agency, Cleveland.

*Gorman Detective Agency, Buffalo, N. Y.

Gorton National Detective Agency, Chicago.

Greensburg Detective Agency, Greensburg, Pa.

Matthew Griffin Co., Philadelphia.

Hallerin Agency, Grand Rapids, Mich.

Hamilton Detective Agency, Pittsburgh.

Hannons Detective Agency, Minneapolis.

The Edward J. Hargrave Secret Service, Chicago.

Harding Detective Agency, Chicago, Ill.

Harris Detective Agency, Pittsburgh.

*Hartford Private Detective Bureau. (*See* Morse Detective and Patrol Service.)

*Edward Z. Holmes Detective Bureau, New York City.

Hoy Detective Bureau, Minneapolis.

*Otis Hulbert, Cleveland, Ohio. (*See* National Corporation Service, Inc.)

*Industrial Council of Washington, Seattle, Wash.

*Industrial Defense Detective Agency, Boston.

*Industrial Investigators and Engineers. (*See* A. A. Ahner Detective Agency.)

Industrial Relations Service, Ltd., New York City.

*International Auxiliary Co., Kenmore, N. Y., Buffalo, N. Y., Hartford, Conn.

*Independent Operation Union, Pittsburgh, Pa.

*Intercity Protective Agency, New York City.

*International Detective Agency, Philadelphia, Pa.

International Detective Service, Minneapolis.

*International Labor Bureau. (*See* R. A. and I. Co.)

*International Library Service. (*See* R. A. and I. Co.)

The International Secret Service Co., Chicago.

Interstate Detective Agency, Chicago.

Jerome Agency, Pittsburgh (headquarters in San Francisco).

Frederick W. Job, expert in labor matters, Marquette Building, Chicago.

*Col. Joseph Johnston (Lake Erie Chemical Co.), Cleveland.

J. Oswald Jones, detective agency, St. Paul.

*A. J. Kane Detective Agency, San Francisco, Calif.

The Kane Service, Chicago.

Kelly-Gleason Detective Agency, Minneapolis (branch office in Des Moines).

Capt. Bernard Kelcher, New York City.

*Kemp Agency, Nason & Roolett, Inc., San Francisco, Calif.

*Keystone Operation Union, Pittsburgh, Pa.

*Keystone State Detective Agency, Philadelphia, Pa.

*Kurty Detective Agency, Wilkes-Barre, Pa.

*Robert Lawrence Detective Agency, Brooklyn, N. Y.

Edmund Leigh, New York City. (*See* National Intelligence Plant Protection Service.)

Madison Detective Bureau, New York City.

*Managers Operation Union, Pittsburgh, Pa.

*Manufacturers' and Merchants' Inspection Bureau. (*See* Howard W. Russell, Inc.)

Manufacturers' Auxiliary Co., Detroit.

Manufacturers' Efficiency Service, Detroit.

Manufacturers' Service, Cleveland. (*See* H. Clay Folger, Schofield Bldg., Cleveland.)

*Ignatius McCarty, San Francisco, Calif.

*McDuff National Detective Agency, Birmingham, Ala.

*G. T. McNulty, Inc., Philadelphia, Pa.

Merchants' Industrial Association, New York City.

Merchants' National Detective Bureau, St. Paul.

*Merchants' Secret Service Corporation, Fort Wayne, Ind.

*Metlers Mutual Agency, Sikeston, Mo.

Metropolitan Agency, Cleveland and Detroit.

Jake Mints Agency, Cleveland.

The Mooney-Boland-Southerland Corporation, Chicago, Detroit, New York City. (*See* Fred C. Mumford Agency.)

*Tommy Moran, Pittsburgh.

*More Detective and Patrol Service, Wilson, Conn.

*Fred C. Mumford Agency (successor to Mooney & Boland), New York City.

The Murphy-McDonnel Secret Service Co., Detroit.

The Murphy Secret Service, Detroit.

McGovern Detective Service, Pittsburgh (special representatives in 20 cities).

McGrath Secret Service Co., 8820 Carnegie Ave., Cleveland.

McGuire & White Agency, Chicago.

McLellan's Detective Bureau, New York City.

Morgan Detective Agency, Boston.

National Mutual Service.

National Manufacturers' Syndicate.

These last two names are used by the personnel and training department of the Sherman Service, Inc. National Manufacturers' Syndicate has its head office in Chicago and recruiting offices at New York City and Boston. Other offices are in Philadelphia, Cleveland, St. Louis, and Toronto.

*National Corporation Service, Inc. (E. E. MacGuffin), Youngstown, Ohio.

*National Corporation Service of La., New Orleans.

*National Detective Agency, Newark, N. J.

National Detective Agency, Detroit.

*National Detective Service, Philadelphia, Pa.

National Erectors' Association, Chicago.

National Founders' Association, Chicago.

National Metal Trades Association, Chicago.

*New Jersey Engineering Corporation.

North American National Detective Bureau, East Minneapolis.

North Western Detective Agency, New York City.

Northern Information Bureau, Minneapolis.

O'Brien & Sons Detective Agency, Chicago.

Captain O'Brien's Detective Agency, New York City.

J. F. O'Brien Detective Agency, Newark, N. J.

Rouse O'Brien, Cincinnati, Ohio.

*O'Connell Detective Agency, 342 Madison Avenue, New York.

*Val O'Farrell Detective Agency (A. B. Ownes), New York City.

O'Neil Secret Service, Detroit.

*Val O'Toole's Detective Agency, New York City. (*See* Pioneer Industrial Service.)

*Pattee Service, St. Louis.

*Forest C. Pendleton, Inc. (*See* R. A. & I. Co.)

*Pennsylvania Industrial Service. (*See* R. A. & I. Co.)

Perkins Union Detective Agency, Pittsburgh.

*Peterson Detective Agency, Pittsburgh.

Pinkerton's National Detective Agency. Offices: New York, Boston, Philadelphia, Los Angeles, Hartford, Syracuse, Baltimore, Atlanta, Buffalo, Montreal, Dallas, Cleveland, Toronto, Pittsburgh, Chicago, Detroit, Cincinnati, Minneapolis, Denver, St. Paul, St. Louis, New Orleans, Richmond, Kansas City, Houston, Providence, San Francisco, Salt Lake City, Spokane, Seattle, Portland, Ore., Indianapolis, Omaha, Milwaukee, Scranton.

*Pioneer Industrial Service, New York City.

Pioneer International Detective Bureau, Minneapolis.

Production Service Co., Cincinnati.

Railway and Industrial Protective Association, Philadelphia and Pittsburgh.
Railway Audit & Inspection Co., Philadelphia and Pittsburgh.
*Pennsylvania Industrial Service.
*Central Industrial Service.
*International Library Service.
*Forest C. Pendleton, Inc.
*International Labor Bureau.
Ray Detective Agency & Merchants' Secret Service, Boston.
Edwin L. Reed & Co., Chicago.
Rhodes Secret Service Bureau, Cleveland.
Dominick G. Riley Detective Bureau, Inc., New York City.
*Teddy Roberts, Pittsburgh and West Virginia.
Howard W. Russell, Inc., or Manufacturers' and Merchants' Inspection Bureau, Milwaukee; industrial department, espionage work in factories.
*Saile-Pierson Detective Agency, Philadelphia.
*Stahl Secret Service, Philadelphia, Pa.
Schindler, Inc., New York City. Handles Sherman's civil and criminal work.
Scott Secret Service, Philadelphia (now Frank L. Scott Detective Agency, Boston).
G. A. Seagrove Co., Chicago.
Shea and Farley Detective Bureau, New York City.
Sherman Service, Inc.
    Offices (headquarters now at New York City): Boston, St. Louis, Philadelphia, Cleveland, Providence, New York, Chicago, New Haven, Detroit.
Shippy-Hunt International Detective Agency, Chicago.
Soule Secret Service, Chicago.
Standard Protection Co., Cleveland.
Standard Secret Service Agency, Detroit.
Standard Service Co., Cleveland.
Stanley Detective Agency, Chicago.
*Sterling Secret Service, Detroit, Mich.
*Carl Swinburne Agency, St. Louis.
Tate's Detective Bureau, Philadelphia.

*Sherwood Detective Bureau. (*See* Eagle Industrial Associates.)
*Smith's Detective Agency, Dallas, Tex.
*Standard Industrial Service, New York, N. Y.
Thiel Detective Service Co., New York City; central office now in Chicago, St. Louis, Mo., St. Paul, other branch offices.
Trotter Detective Bureau, Minneapolis.
*Elsie M. Tunison, Detroit, Mich.
*T. R. Turner, New York.
William J. Turner Detective Agency, Chicago.
*United Detective Bureau, New York City.
*United Detective Service, San Francisco, Calif.
United Service Co., Cleveland.
Waddell-Mahon Agency, New York City.
Washington Detective Agency, New York City.
Washington Service Bureau, New York City (Jack Cohen, A. D. Cohen).
*Watkins Jacobs Detective Agency, Youngstown, Ohio.
*Watts & Whelan, Detroit, Mich.
Western Construction Co., Chicago.
*C. R. Williams Investigating Bureau, New York City.
Williams Agency, Boston.
Wilson's Detective Agency, Milwaukee.
Daniel Wolff Agency, New York City.
*Wood Service System, 1228 Ninety-first Street, New York City.
Young's Detective Agency, New York City.
— *Prelim.*, *p. 72 ff.*

B.

Type of spy report received by Mr. Weckler of the Chrysler Corp.

SPECIAL REPORT COVERING MEETING OF DELEGATES OF THE UNITED AUTOMOBILE WORKERS (A. F. OF L.) AND AFFILIATED UNIONS, HELD TUESDAY, JULY 7TH, 1936

A special meeting of local officers of the

United Automobile Workers and delegates and officers of the Automotive Industrial Workers Association, Mechanics Educational Society and Associated Automobile Workers of America, was held Tuesday evening, July 7th, at A.I.W.A. headquarters, 8944 Jos Campau Avenue, with an attendance of about 60 officers and delegates.

Richard Frankensteen acted as chairman. Arthur Greer served as secretary.

The first question brought before the meeting was in connection with straightening out the list of delegates that were selected to serve on the District Organizing Committee at a previous meeting, held Tuesday evening, June 30th. At that meeting there was much confusion as to who was appointed to the committee and in some cases delegates were appointed to the committee and did not know it while in other cases certain delegates believed they were on the committee but found out later on that they were mistaken.

This evening a complete list of the temporary Organizing Committee of 21 was made known as follows:

George Wilson, Dodge
"Red" Miller, Mixed Local #155 (formerly M. E. S.)
Cliff Zimmerman, Dodge
Arthur Greer, Hudson Motor
Gould, Murray Body
R. Thomas, Chrysler (Kercheval)
Reuther, Ternstedts
Hindle, Kelsey Wheel
McKie, Ford Motor
Willis, Motor Products
Ayers, Graham-Paige
Andrews, Dodge
Loyd Jones, Motor Products
Maurice Fields, Dodge
J. Kennedy, Chrysler
Barber, Fisher Body Local #157 (formerly M. E. S.)
Berry, Zenith Carburetor
Coleman, Herron-Zimmer Molding Co.

A letter prepared by Seymour, an officer of the transmission department district local (Dodge), was read, in which Seymour suggested that members of organized labor should confine their purchases as much as possible to merchandise bearing the union label. He explained in his letter that many members of organized labor overlook entirely the union label program and soon fall into the habit of buying merchandise that is made under "unfair open shop" conditions.

The only comment made about this letter was when the delegates agreed to carry out this recommendation as closely as possible.

Secretary Arthur Greer read some prepared statements issued at the time Mayor Tenerowicz of Hamtramck was a candidate for election this year. According to the statement read by Greer, Mayor Tenerowicz in his campaign for the office of Mayor, stated that if elected to office, he would see that the Hamtramck Police Department would not interfere with peaceful picketing or escort "strike breakers" to a plant and in fact would keep the Police Department out of the strike as long as the strikers did not resort to destruction of private property. Also in this statement, that Greer read, Mayor Tenerowicz stated that he would also stop the Police Department from interfering with the distribution of handbills around the plants.

Following the reading of this letter, Frankensteen remarked that the Hamtramck Police are interfering to some extent with the distribution of handbills. During the discussion that followed, it was agreed to send a typewritten copy of these statements, made during the election campaign this year, to Mayor Tenerowicz and another copy to the Hamtramck Police Department. Also copies will be mimeographed later on and sent out to all members of the United Automobile Workers, especially members of local unions in Hamtramck. . . .

Frankensteen said during the past week he has talked upon several occasions to small groups of Fisher Body employees of the Piquette Avenue plant, having met them nearby in beer gardens and restaurants, and his contacts indicate that these men are deeply interested in organization and all that is necessary to bring them into the folds of organized labor is some constructive work on the part of the organizers. Frankensteen said he intends to keep in touch with the Fisher Body employees and will assist the organizers in preparing meetings and will also speak at these gatherings.

Frankensteen announced that a series of four mass meetings will be held in different sections of the city, commencing on Thursday evening of this week. He said on Thursday, July 9th, the first of these mass meetings will be held at Chandler Park and included among the speakers will be Adolph Germer, the personal representative of John L. Lewis and his Committee for Industrial Organization. He explained this mass meeting is being held especially for employees of Chrysler, Hudson Motor, Zenith Carburetor, Motor Products, Briggs, Budd Wheel, Bower Roller Bearing, Freuhauf Trailer, Federal Mogul, Bohn Aluminum, Acme Die Cast and Detroit Vapor Stover. He said the mass meeting next week will probably be held in Hamtramck and efforts will be made to secure the Rosinski Stadium, at the corner of Jos. Campau Avenue and Dan Street. He explained that it is not certain if this stadium can be rented and the exact date of the meeting next week has not been decided upon. He said this, however, will be announced later this week over the radio broadcasts on Friday, and Saturday on Station WMBC. In this connection, Frankensteen explained that the United Automobile Workers have secured time on Station WMBC on Friday evenings from 10:15 P. M. to 10:30 P. M. and on Saturday evenings from 7:15 P. M. to 7:30 P. M. He said both of the programs this week will be in English, but arrangements are being made to broadcast a Polish program on either Friday or Saturday of next week and hopes to have Leo Kryzki, speak. Kryzki is Vice-President of the Amalgamated Clothing Workers, one of the International Unions that composes the Committee for Industrial Organization.

Frankensteen announced that International President Homer Martin of the United Automobile Workers visited Washington last week and spent considerable time with John L. Lewis and completed arrangements for the International Union of the United Automobile Workers to join with the Lewis Committee for Industrial Organization. He said the United Rubber Workers has also joined the Committee for Industrial Organization and this makes 12 International Unions that are represented on the committee.

Frankensteen said Martin returned to Detroit yesterday but left for Pittsburgh today where he will meet with the organizers in the steel drive and other members of the Committee for Industrial Organization, for the purpose of making definite arrangements to send four or five organizers to Detroit and also arrange for financial aid and work out other details in connections with launching a drive in the auto industry. Frankensteen said he understands that four or perhaps five organizers from the Committee for Industrial Organization will be sent to Detroit in about two weeks. Frankensteen stated that this coming organizing drive in the auto industry will be carried on under the supervision and direction of the Committee for Industrial Organization.

In his concluding remarks, Frankensteen stated that handbills have been prepared announcing a meeting to be held at Chandler Park on Thursday evening, July 9th and explained that these leaflets will be distributed around the East Side plants on Wednesday and Thursday. He said delegates present this evening who are employed in East Side shops might find an opportunity to carry a few of these handbills inside and distribute them to some of their friends.

Following Frankensteen's talk, there was some general discussion in which most of the delegates took part. This was to the effect that the women folks and wives of union members are not supporting the union properly. It was argued that many of the wives object to their husbands attending meetings, on the grounds that after the meetings are over they visit beer gardens and other amusement places and do not get home until one or two o'clock in the morning. During the discussion, it was admitted that many members took advantage of the union meetings to have a "night out" and this has become known to many of the women folk, with the result that many members complain that their wives put up serious objection whenever they want to attend a union meeting.

Frankensteen brought his discussion to an end by explaining that he will arrange for a special radio program for the women folks and explain to them how necessary it is for their husbands to attend union meetings if a successful organization of auto workers is to be set up.

James Foster, who has been very active in the Automotive Industrial Workers Association, declared that right now would be a very favorable time to put forth some real organizing efforts directed toward the Briggs employees. Foster explained that Briggs owns the Detroit Tigers Baseball Club and if a strike should develop at the Briggs Plant during the course of organization, then Navin

Field could be picketed. He said this organizing drive of course would have to take place during the baseball season. The other delegates present this evening apparently did not think much of Foster's suggestion because no other comment was made.

It was very warm in the hall this evening and many of the delegates complained about the heat, with the result that Chairman Frankensteen adjourned the meeting at 9:30 P. M.

SPECIAL REPORT

R–C:D–88
7—8—36

The above information, obtained from sources deemed reliable, is furnished without responsibility on the part of this company.

— *IV, p. 1389 ff.*

C.

Report of Burns Operative, Robert W. Coates, on a union organization meeting which he attended, and in which he took an active part:

PITTSBURGH, PA.,
(*Saturday*), *July 15th, 1933.*
Pittsburgh Operator No. 8062
Pittsburgh Investigator C–24 Reports:

Having been instructed by Acting Manager D. R. S. to wait at the Agency Office, I there met Pittsburgh Investigator D–1 and Mr. Morrow. I was instructed to accompany Investigator D–1 to the vicinity of the McGeagh Building where those identified with the bakery industry were to have a meeting. I was instructed to endeavor to be admitted to the meeting and ascertain what transpired.

At 7:30 P. M. I left the Agency Office accompanied by Pittsburgh Investigator D–1 and when at an appropriate distance from the McGeagh Building, we separated.

Approaching the McGeagh Building, I observed several men who were no doubt active in unionism, closely observing all those who were entering the building. Watching my opportunity I managed to go into the building immediately in the rear of three other men who had inquired if there was a meeting in the building. The watcher at the front of the building advised us the meeting was in the room in the rear of the third floor of the building.

I followed up the stairs to the third floor and observed several men in the third floor hall closely observing all men that entered the rear room where the meeting was to be held.

After entering I counted the number of men present and found there were seventy-eight young and older men in the room. Several of the younger men especially appeared to be truck drivers. In fact the majority appeared to be those employed in distribution rather than in the manufacturing end.

Seated up front at the chairman's table was an Irishman whom they all appeared to refer to as Dan, although one man present in the hall advised me he was Mr. Metche. Seated to the left of the chairman's table was a man they all addressed as Sam, a Jew, possibly Russian Jew, who has evidently been in this country for some time, as he spoke very good English, had exceptionally good diction, and a very forceful fellow of about 35 years of age. Later I learned that Sam was the Business Agent and that Metche was President of the Bakers Union.

At the opening of the meeting Metche addressed the men as non-union men and stated that he was very much gratified at seeing so many present. Metche went on to explain that he and Sam had been very active in the past two weeks in trying to interview as many men employed in bakeries about Pittsburgh as they could and that he did not expect to see so many

present. (At this time there were several more men entering the room. Later additions brought the total number to over one hundred men present.)

Metche advised the men that the Industrial Recovery Act recently passed had made it possible for the men to secure their rights and proper recognition with their employers and that they desired to unionize the baking industry as a whole, taking in every one employed about the shop whether he be a truck driver, baker or shop man, salesman, and in fact all those employed in the baking industry. He stated that he observed one shop represented one hundred per cent and I inquired from one of the men and learned that he had reference to the men from the Hankey Baking Company.

After the usual organizers speech pointing out to the men what benefits unionism would give them if they joined, Metche introduced the Business Agent as "Sam" the Business Agent, who would also address the men. There appeared to be some significance in the manner in which reference was made to this man and that by addressing them by their Christian name.

Business Agent Sam then addressed the men urging them to join the union. He stated the initial cost would be $5.00 to join and $2.25 per month dues for beneficiary members and $1.40 per month for non-beneficiary members. In case of death of a beneficiary member, his beneficiary would receive $300.00, and in case his wife died, he would receive $75.00.

Sam stated there had been deep inroads made in the ranks of the union bakers and that he had learned the Master Bakers were preparing their Code to submit to Gen. Hugh S. Johnson, Recovery Administrator and that they had decided on asking for a forty hour week with a minimum wage of $20.00 per week with proportionate wages accordingly and he wanted all the men to join so that the Bakers Union could show at least 75% unionism and demand a thirty hour week with a $30.00 minimum wage. Some young fellow stated in interruption that he only earned twelve dollars a week. Sam went on to explain to the men that he felt confident that if a sufficient number joined it would only be a matter of another month when they could demand this or close up the shops.

Sam then urged the men to come forward and sign a pink application blank to join the union. The men did not rush to do so and considerable comment surged through the men in the room. I suggested to one man who remarked to me that he did not know whether there was anyone from his shop that was spotting and he was not going to take any chances on losing his job as he had not been working very steady. I suggested that he suggest that the application blanks be passed around to each man in the room and let him take it home and decide to do what he wanted. This was overheard by a young man, who took it up from the floor and this was done. I received one of the blanks.

At this juncture the men were displaying considerable concern over the initiation fee demanded and there was considerable discussion among the different groups and mixing in I suggested that as I had only worked eight days out at Hallers I did not have the money to spare but that my idea would be to take all the old union members in that had dropped out free of any back dues and all the new members at some nominal sum such as a dollar in order to get each and every man. One man who is very likely a union man advised me that my suggestion would have to go before the executive board. I argued my point and stated that if they want to get all the men in my idea would not work a hardship on those like myself who had

been out of employment so long, also pointing out that this was labor's opportunity with the cooperation of the government that the labor movement has never had in its history. My point seemed to carry and the union men took the matter up with Sam and Sam came to my chair and pointed out that funds were needed to defray expenses. I offset this by stating that it did not cost near as much to represent a million men than it did a thousand as quicker results can be obtained if the initiation expense was totally cut out as it was quantity in numbers that was required now in a very limited time and that when the men did sign up strong to say 85 or 90% it would only be a month when the dues would be pouring in and the desired result would be the same, regardless as to whether the $5.00 was paid in or not.

Sam got my point and then advised the men that if they could not spare the $5.00 to turn in $1.00 with their application and he would take the matter up with the executive board and know more about what their action would be at the next meeting to be held the first week in August. This went over pretty good and an elderly man paid in one dollar for himself and five dollars for five others. When Sam saw that this was going over so well he again came to my chair and asked me for my application and I advised him of my financial circumstances pointing out to him that as I had just been employed at Hallers Bakery only eight days ago and did not know all the men and was afraid there might be someone spotting in the room, I would rather mail my application in. I advised Sam there was no doubt in my mind that several others felt just like I did and Sam then went on to declare to all the men that another good point had been brought up and that while arrangements had been made to stop any spotters coming to the meeting and he was confident there were none present, it was possible there were men in the room who desired to join and were afraid they might lose their jobs but if they desired to do so they could fill out their own application blank and mail it to him and he assured all those present that he and no one else would know who joined until the organization was complete, and the records then turned over to their secretary, to be elected later by them.

Sam and Metche finally enlisted what I would estimate about forty members and at the $1.00 fee but it is quite likely that at least another 20% more would sign their application and mail it in.

During the filling out of the applications the men milled about the room and I met Sam later when he inquired of me as to my name. I gave him a name and advised him that I would very likely send in my name, but desired more secrecy as I did not wish to lose my job, which appeared to satisfy him. Sam states he was well pleased with what applications he had received and looked for a large meeting the first week in August.

Metche then addressed the men advising them that while they could take what papers they had received home with them, he desired that all the men keep it very confidential as to what had gone on tonight and not by any chance discuss the meeting in their shops as he wanted all the men to join and that much better results could be obtained if the matter were kept secret until the shops were fully organized. He stated further that he desired each man to work for a 100% organization and urged the men to bring some new men to the next meeting.

Metche further stated that organization work was going on all over the country in all trades to enable their representatives of each respective industry to show a strong hand when the code for each industry is finally settled on and it behooves every wage earner to join now and show a united front in each separate industry.

Each man present was urged to read the daily papers about the Industrial Recovery Act and see for himself what a wonderful opportunity the wage earner has today which he has never had before, describing the Industrial Recovery Act as a new "Bill of Rights."

By this time several groups of men were leaving the room and continuing on downstairs and I went down to the front of the building where I met several congregated about the doorway. Mixing in the discussion I could readily observe that Sam and Metche had planted strong arguments in fertile ground. While taking part in the discussion Sam came down looking and inquiring for a fellow he called "Lampel" who works out at Hallers Bakery. Not knowing Lampel I told Sam so, whereupon he stated he was very anxious to have seen him before he got away, indicating he was at the meeting and had left. I took this opportunity to properly introduce myself and compliment Sam in his masterful manner in handling his subject tonight, but while Sam shook hands with me he stated he was "Sam" and desired to see me at the next meeting. I told him that I expected to be present if I was still working and hoped he had success in securing 100% organization. Sam stated he was very grateful for the attendance tonight and someone in the crowd asked Sam where he was from and Sam replied "somewhere in Europe" and grinned.

I joined several of the men in having refreshments at a nearby restaurant and observed Pittsburgh Investigator D-1 in the vicinity. Later I left the vicinity of the McGeagh Bldg. and joined Investigator D-1 when we both reported in person to Mr. Morrow at his residence on Union Ave., N. S.

Mr. Morrow instructed me to report at their office Monday morning at 10:00

o'clock when he desired me to confer with him and others regarding future plans.

I left Mr. Morrow at 11:00 P. M., returned to my room where I was engaged until 3:00 A. M. preparing this report. After doing so I discontinued for the day.

Expenses:

Supper and lunch.......... $1.00

Refreshments..............	1.20
Car fare...................	.10
Time: One day..............	12.00
	$14.30

MH/

—VIII, pp. 3119–3122

D.

Members of Employers' Association of Akron and amounts of their contributions, 1933 to 1936:

	1933	*1934*	*1935*	*1936*
B. F. Goodrich Co. 500 S. Main Street..............	$6220.70	$9216.01	$10868.64	$11117.52
Goodyear Tire & Rubber Co. 1144 E. Market Street..........	$6876.72	$11266.69	$13988.31	$13792.00
Firestone Tire & Rubber Co. 1278 S. Main Street.............	$4372.45	$7271.00	$9152.96	$9419.44
General Tire & Rubber Co. E. Market & Holmes St.........	$728.55	$1047.72	$1284.56	$1222.64
Mohawk Rubber Co. 1235 Second Avenue............	$279.05	$293.35	$206.30	$158.90
American Hard Rubber Co. Seiberling Street................	$207.30	$215.75	$220.45	$246.70
Quaker Oats Co. 102 S. Howard Street...........	$342.65	$367.20	$342.25	$347.35
Robinson Clay Products Co. 1100 2nd National Bldg.........	$6.00	$33.50	$36.00	$36.00
Akers & Harpham Co. 1065 Dublin Street.............	$3.00	$5.75	$6.00	$3.00
Thos. Phillips Co. 23 W. Exchange Street..........	$50.50	$58.00	$60.10	$60.00
Carmichael Construction Co. 148 E. Miller Avenue...........	$8.35	$8.00	None	None
Imperial Electric Co. 64 Ira Avenue.................	$26.75	$26.50	$30.90	$39.40
National Rubber Machinery Co. 917 Sweitzer Avenue............	$123.30	$126.10	$82.35	$85.25
Akron Equipment Co. E. Exchange & Annadale........	$21.75	$34.25	$30.90	$32.40
Mechanical Mold & Machine Co. 946 S. High Street..............	$53.15	$57.65	$64.20	$63.70
Akron Standard Mold Co. 1624 Englewood Avenue........:.	$84.80	$90.75	$85.40	$82.75

Walter F. Kirn
  366 S. Broadway............... $2.60 $2.75 $2.45 $1.65
Resigned February, 1933:
  Steigner-Koch Co.
    99 W. Market Street........ $.40   ....
Resigned June, 1936:
  Franklin Brothers Co.
    49 E. Glenwood Ave........ $6.65 $9.40 $10.55 $2.85

I hereby certify that the above is a true and correct list of the members of The Employers' Association of Akron & Vicinity from January 1st, 1933, up to the present date, and that the amounts set opposite their names for the years mentioned are the true and correct amounts contributed by them respectively to the Association in dues for said years and that there have been no other contributions.

H. C. Parsons, *Sec'y-Treas.*

— *VIII, pp. 3202, 3203*

E.

Sample detailed report sent by The Goodyear Co. to Mr. Cowdrick, secretary of the special conference committee:

THE GOODYEAR TIRE
& RUBBER COMPANY,
Akron, Ohio, June 12, 1936.
Mr. E. S. COWDRICK,
30 Rockefeller Plaza,
New York City, N. Y.

DEAR MR. COWDRICK: We have sent you some newspaper reports the last few days covering reports of the labor situation at Gadsden and its effect upon our local situation here in Akron. We have just received a report from a representative of our management in Gadsden on this situation which we believe will be of interest.

Dalrymple, President of the Rubberworkers Union, talked with our local superintendent in Gadsden late Friday (June 5) and apparently was satisfied with the explanation given him regarding the dismissal of two union employees. Both of these dismissals were caused by violation of company rules. One employee had spoiled considerable stock and had tried to cover up same. The other one had been repeatedly warned as to garnisheements, but had persisted in not looking after his outside financial affairs, and just recently was found guilty of some other loose financial deals in regards to issuing of checks.

While in Gadsden, Dalrymple called a meeting in the Court House, at which he was the chief speaker. The meeting was attended by a large group, including most of the union people in town. Of this union organization there were a large number from one of the local textile plants who were out of a job. There also were some members present from a steel company, as well as some from our own plant.

The statement was made by the speaker that there were a number of dissatisfied workers in the Goodyear plant and when he was asked from the floor who was dissatisfied and who had asked him to come to Gadsden, his explanation was met by a shower of eggs, tomatoes and rocks. A free-for-all fight was precipitated and a few knives and guns were drawn by some of the radical union members. No one was seriously injured, however, and the

Sheriff escorted Dalrymple out the back entrance of the Court House.

As he came down the steps and started across the street a gang of men rushed up, and between this point and his hotel he was rather roughly treated.

His wife was at the hotel and they were told to leave the town and not return to Alabama again.

During the mixup one of the union men had flourished his gun, and some of the non-union workers, when he reported for work Monday morning, asked if he was still armed. When he replied that he was not, one of the men in the shop proceeded to give him a good beating. This precipitated some difficulty, and when the supervision were able to break up the trouble, they escorted a number of the principals to the gatehouse to give them a chance to cool off.

After investigation, the supervision found there were other union men on the other shift who were going to be given the same treatment by non-union workers, and so these clock cards were pulled.

14 employes out of a total of 20 were given their pay. This 14 includes the original two who were dismissed. The other 12 were paid off with the understanding that their working in the plant might cause trouble and they were advised to stay out for some time, but they were not formally discharged.

Federal and State investigators have been to Gadsden and yesterday afternoon we were visited by a committee of the Rubberworkers' Union to discuss this Gadsden difficulty and also the dismissal of a man at the Kelly Springfield Plant.

At this meeting we were presented with an agreement similar to the one which was discussed at the settlement of the strike here in Akron. Also, there was tacked on it a clause that we would agree to pay the same rates of pay in both Gadsden and Cumberland that we are paying in Akron. The management informed the Committee that they were not in a position to consider this agreement but would investigate the cases of the men at the Gadsden Plant as well as the one at Kelly Springfield.

This situation, of course, has been the cause of some difficulty here in Akron. It resulted in complete cessation of operations Wednesday midnight. There was some further trouble in the Plant II Pit because the union workers would not work with some of the non-union employes in their department.

The situation yesterday was rather tense because of the announcement of the future policy that no minimum wage would be paid in the future to anyone whose earnings were affected by a sit-down, nor would minimum wage be paid to any employee who reported for work and were unable to work because of a sitdown.

At the meeting yesterday afternoon, however, the union committee discussed this new policy with the management and seemed to understand it and abide by it if we would agree to clean up a couple of wage matters caused by the difficulty on Thursday morning at Plant II. This was cleaned up to the satisfaction of all concerned and we got by last night without any difficulty.

We will keep you informed as to any further developments.

Yours very truly,
L. A. HURLEY,
Manager, Inter Plant Relations.
L A Hurley
TA

— *VIII, pp. 3206, 3207*

F.

Frankensteen's account of the attack on him by Ford service men:

Walter and I walked up and photographers called and asked to take a picture.

They took a picture of the three of us, Walter, Jack Kennedy and myself. Immediately after the picture was taken a fellow came over and said, "you are on Ford property, get the hell off of here." We started to walk for the steps to leave, but I hadn't taken three steps when I felt a crack in the back of the neck. I turned around and as I turned more blows were struck. As I started to defend myself they got me on all sides. There seemed to be about 25 men working on me.

Participating in the attack on the bridge were about 150 men. I was knocked down, but someone grabbed my coat from the back and threw it over my head. They knocked me down again, turned me over on my side and began to kick me in the stomach. When I would protect my side they would kick my head.

One of the attackers would say, "That is enough, let him go." Then they would pick me up and stand me on my feet, but I was no sooner on my feet than they would knock me down again. This went on about five times. They let me lie there for a while; during that time every once in a while someone would grind his heel into me. They pulled my legs apart and kicked me in the scrotum. By this time they had me driven to the steps, leading down on the east side of the bridge. As I started down the first step I was again knocked down. They picked me up and bounced me from one step to the next. I was bounced on each step. As I went down four or five steps I came to the landing.

There were four or five more men who proceeded to administer the blows from that place. This continued until they had me on the cinders by the street car tracks on the south side of the fence. At that point a street car approached. The men began bouncing me on the cinders, picking me up and knocking me down on the cinders.

I lost consciousness while on the bridge, but when they stood me on my feet it seemed to restore my faculties. I knew what was going on but could not speak.

They said, "Go get your coat." My coat was lying on the street car tracks. A big fat fellow, a man I could identify easily, as his face is very pronounced in my mind, said, "Go get your coat." As I went to pick up my coat I was again knocked down. That was the last time that I was knocked down. By this time I had approached the end of the fence where we were picked up by newspaper men who drove us to a physician's office.

During this time the Dearborn police who were present made no effort to forestall this action.

United Automobile Worker,
May 29, 1937.
(Reprinted by permission.)

G.

Description of suppressed Paramount News Reel of the "Memorial Day Massacre" in South Chicago:

The St. Louis Post-Dispatch was the first newspaper in the United States to print the following account and thereafter it was reprinted by many other newspapers.

Senators See Suppressed Movie of Chicago Police Killing Steel Strikers

Brutal Scenes of Memorial Day Vividly Shown in News Reel

Members of Investigating Committee Shocked at Picture of Officers Firing Pointblank Into Crowd of Marchers

PURSUED, CLUBBED DOWN AS THEY RUN

Audience Views Close-Ups of Encounter, Accompanied by Sounds of Shots and Screams of Wounded Demonstrators

Post-Dispatch Bureau.
201–205 Kellogg Bldg.
(Copyright, 1937, Pulitzer Publishing Co.)
WASHINGTON, June 16. — Five agents of the La Follette Civil Liberties Committee, headed by Robert Wohlforth, the committee's secretary, arrived in Chicago yesterday to begin an investigation of the tragic events of Memorial day, when nine persons were killed or fatally wounded by city police in smashing an attempt by steel strike demonstrators to march past the Republic Steel Co. plant in South Chicago.

Appearance of the committee's agents on the scene coincided with the death of the ninth victim, a 17-year-old boy reported to have joined the pickets in the hope of getting a job in the mill after settlement of the strike.

It was learned today that the committee's decision to proceed with the inquiry was hastened by the private showing here last week of a suppressed news reel, in which the police attack on the demonstrators is graphically recorded. The committee obtained possession of the film in New York, after its maker, the Paramount Co., had announced that it would not be exhibited publicly, for fear of inciting riots throughout the country.

Senators Shocked by Scenes

The showing of the film here was conducted with the utmost secrecy. The audience was almost limited to Senators La Follette (Prog.), Wisconsin, and Thomas (Dem.), Utah, who compose the committee, and members of the staff. Those who saw it were shocked and amazed by scenes showing scores of uniformed policemen firing their revolvers pointblank into a dense crowd of men, women and children, and then pursuing and clubbing the survivors unmercifully as they made frantic efforts to escape.

The impression produced by these fearful scenes was heightened by the sound record which accompanies the picture, reproducing the roar of police fire and the screams of the victims. It was run off several times for the scrutiny of the investigators, and at each showing they detected additional instances of "frightfulness." It is expected to be of extraordinary value in identifying individual policemen and their victims. The film itself evidently is an outstanding example of camera reporting under difficult conditions.

Description of Picture

The following description of the picture comes from a person who saw it several times, and had a particular interest in studying it closely for detail. Its accuracy is beyond question.

The first scenes show police drawn up in a long line across a dirt road which runs diagonally through a large open field before turning into a street which is parallel to, and some 200 yards distant from, the high fence surrounding the Republic mill. The police line extends 40 or 50 yards on each side of the dirt road. Behind the line, and in the street beyond, nearer the mill, are several patrol wagons and numerous reserve squads of police.

Straggling across the field, in a long, irregular line, headed by two men carrying American flags, the demonstrators are shown approaching. Many carry placards. They appear to number about 300 — approximately the same as the police — although it is known that some 2000 strike sympathizers were watching the march from a distance.

Marchers Halted by Police

A vivid close-up shows the head of the parade being halted at the police line. The flag-bearers are in front. Behind them the placards are massed. They bear such devices as: "Come on Out — Help Win the Strike"; "Republic vs. the People," and "C I O." Between the flag-bearers is the marchers' spokesman, a muscular young man in shirt-sleeves, with a C I O button on the band of his felt hat.

He is arguing earnestly with a police officer who appears to be in command. His vigorous gestures indicate that he is insisting on permission to continue through the police line, but in the general din of yelling and talking his words cannot be distinguished. His expression is serious, but no suggestion of threat or violence is apparent. The police officer, whose back is to the camera, makes one impatient gesture of refusal, and says something which cannot be understood.

Then suddenly, without apparent warning, there is a terrific roar of pistol shots, and men in the front ranks of the marchers go down like grass before a scythe. The camera catches approximately a dozen falling simultaneously in a heap. The massive, sustained roar of the police pistols lasts perhaps two or three seconds.

Police Charge With Sticks

Instantly the police charge on the marchers with riot sticks flying. At the same time tear gas grenades are seen sailing into the mass of demonstrators, and clouds of gas rise over them. Most of the crowd is now in flight. The only discernible case of resistance is that of a marcher with a placard on a stick, which he uses in an attempt to fend off a charging policeman. He is successful for only an instant. Then he goes down under a shower of blows.

The scenes which follow are among the most harrowing of the picture. Although the ground is strewn with dead and wounded, and the mass of the marchers are in precipitate flight down the dirt road and across the field, a number of individuals, either through foolish hardihood, or because they have not yet realized what grim and deadly business is in progress around them, have remained behind, caught in the midst of the charging police.

In a manner which is appallingly businesslike, groups of policemen close in on these isolated individuals, and go to work on them with their clubs. In several instances, from two to four policemen are seen beating one man. One strikes him horizontally across the face, using his club as he would wield a baseball bat. Another crashes it down on top of his head, and still another is whipping him across the back.

These men try to protect their heads with their arms, but it is only a matter of a second or two until they go down. In one such scene, directly in the foreground, a policeman gives the fallen man a final smash on the head, before moving on to the next job.

In the front line during the parley with the police is a girl, not more than five feet tall, who can hardly weigh more than 100 pounds. Under one arm she is carrying a purse and some newspapers. After the first deafening volley of shots she turns, to find that her path to flight is blocked by a heap of fallen men. She stumbles over them, apparently dazed.

The scene shifts for a moment, then she is seen going down under a quick blow from a policeman's club, delivered from behind. She gets up, and staggers around. A few moments later she is shown being shoved into a patrol wagon, as blood cascades down her face and spreads over her clothing.

Straggler's Futile Flight

Preceding this episode, however, is a scene which, for sheer horror, outdoes the rest. A husky, middle-aged, bare-headed man has found himself caught far behind the rear ranks of the fleeing marchers. Between him and the others, policemen are as thick as flies, but he elects to run the gantlet. Astonishingly agile for one of his age and build, he runs like a deer, leaping a ditch, dodging as he goes. Surprised policemen take hasty swings as he passes them. Some get him on the back, some on the back of the head, but he keeps his feet, and keeps going.

The scene is bursting with a frightful sort of drama. Will he make it? The suspense is almost intolerable to those who watch. It begins to look as if he will get through. But no! The police in front have turned around, now, and are waiting for him. Still trying desperately, he swings to the right. He has put his hands up, and is holding them high above his head as he runs.

It is no use. There are police on the right. He is cornered. He turns, still holding high his hands. Quickly the bluecoats close in, and the night sticks fly — above his head, from the sides, from the rear. His upraised arms fall limply under the flailing blows, and he slumps to the ground in a twisting fall, as the clubs continue to rain on him.

C I O officers report that when one of the victims was delivered at an undertaking establishment, it was found that his brains literally had been beaten out, his skull crushed by blows.

Man Paralyzed by Bullet

Ensuing scenes are hardly less poignant. A man shot through the back is paralyzed from the waist. Two policemen try to make him stand up, to get into a patrol wagon, but when they let him go his legs crumple, and he falls with his face in the dirt, almost under the rear step of the wagon. He moves his head and arms, but his legs are limp. He raises his head like a turtle, and claws the ground.

A man over whose white shirt front the blood is spreading perceptibly, is dragged to the side of the road. Two or three policemen bend over and look at him closely. One of them shakes his head, and slips a newspaper under the wounded man's head. There is a plain intimation that he is dying. A man in civilian clothing comes up, feels his pulse a moment then drops the hand, and walks away. Another, in a uniform which might be that of a company policeman, stops an instant, looks at the prostrate figure, and continues on his way.

Loading Wounded in Wagons

The scene shifts to the patrol wagons in the rear. Men with bloody heads, bloody faces, bloody shirts, are being loaded in. One who apparently has been shot in the leg, drags himself painfully into the picture with the aid of two policemen. An elderly man, bent almost double, holding one hand on the back of his head, clambers painfully up the steps and slumps onto the seat, burying his face in both hands. The shoulders of his white shirt are drenched with blood.

There is continuous talking, but it is difficult to distinguish anything, with one exception — out of the babble there rises this clear and distinct ejaculation: "God Almighty!"

The camera shifts back to the central scene. Here and there is a body sprawled in what appears to be the grotesque indifference of death. Far off toward the outer corner of the field, whence they had come originally, the routed marchers are still in flight, with an irregular line of policemen in close pursuit. It is impossible to discern, at this distance, whether violence has ended.

A policeman, somewhat disheveled, his coat open, a scowl on his face, approaches another who is standing in front of the camera. He is sweaty and tired. He says something indistinguishable. Then his face breaks into a sudden grin, he makes a motion of dusting off his hands, and strides away. The film ends.

H.

Blaine Owen's account of the attack on him by T.C.I. thugs:

NIGHT RIDE IN BIRMINGHAM

Birmingham is hot. The air breathes steel, coal, and oil. There are names which should be put in parentheses after the name Birmingham: TCI, Republic Steel, Schloss-Sheffield. And the greatest of these is TCI. TCI is Tennessee Coal and Iron — United States Steel, the House of Morgan.

In the company houses they have established a rule that workers with gardens must not grow corn or anything as high as a man's head. Lights burn in the spaces between the houses all night. Don't be found in the streets after nine-thirty. But somehow the meetings go on, somehow no terror can stop these meetings. Although it means jail and beating, leaflets appear miraculously on doorsteps overnight, calling for organization and struggle.

It was on my way home that a police car went by slowly, two uniformed men in the front seat. One drove, the other swung the spotlight full on me. Across the street stood a dark sedan, men standing about it, smoking. I walked on around the corner. They closed in, and the Ford sedan quietly rolled in front of us, the doors already open. Not a person in the entire block. There was no sense in yelling for help.

Held firmly between them in the back of the car, we shot past the traffic light and between the rows of quiet buildings. No one said a word. The windows were closed tight and we all sweated slowly, out of breath from the tussle, panting . . .

Smash! It came — though I had known it would come — as a surprise. My lip was numb as I took a deep breath and tried to double up as it came again. This time it caught me on the cheek and I could feel the small surface of a yellow gold ring crushing the skin against the bone.

There was a salt taste to the thick blood, and I sucked it in with my breath. A sharp knee dug into my stomach and I gasped, straining to free my arms. I thought I would never again get air into my lungs, they felt crushed and splattered all over inside me. Somehow I forgot my face. It was in my lap maybe, maybe in his lap, a trip-hammer pounding on it, but it was no longer part of me. I started once more in my mind to go carefully through each pocket in my coat, my trousers, the one in my shirt. Suddenly the blows had stopped. The realization startled me and I opened my eyes, but only the right one would open . . .

Another short silence, then he moved once, and his knees came crashing up into my face. "Blaine Owen," he said. "Think you're smart, don't you. Blaine Owen." He dragged it out, gloating over the name, over the victim, like a jackal.

"You've got too much hair you God damn nigger lover," he said, and hauled me into a headlock, my face in his lap. His companion beat a tattoo on my ribs with his doubled fists.

"How do you like this?" he wanted to know, the sound coming choked and jagged from somewhere deep in his throat

as a handful of hair was torn out and stuffed into the thick blood clogging my mouth. I said nothing. There was nothing to say . . .

The tall gaunt one stood in the shadow with the dull gleam of a revolver at his side, and asked me quick short questions. Each time he would pause long enough for the younger one with the straight dark brows and the rolling lips to slam me in the face. "He won't talk," he said. Smash! "Hasn't said a God damn word." Smash! . . . Keep your mouth shut, I said to myself over and over, keep your mouth shut, because they're going to finish you anyway, and the more you say, the more they'll pound before they finish you off.

"Throw him in the river," the fair young one said, and from somewhere a rope was brought.

It must have been the driver, whom I never saw except for the back of his low, broad head there in the car, who pulled my coat off from behind, while the rope cut down across my shoulders, with a high, crying swish before the sharp slap. I felt hands rip off the shirt strip by strip, yanking it off the places where blood had begun to dry and stick. Someone was ripping my trousers with a knife.

Lying face down on the ground I pretended I had passed out, and wondered why I hadn't. The rope cut across my back and at first I clamped my teeth together and it was all right. After the rope bit into the open places time after time, I kept saying to myself, "Throw me in the river, go ahead, bump me off." It gave me something to concentrate on. The whip came down taking bits of skin with it.

The whipping stopped, and a boot crashed into my ribs. I rolled over and slumped back on my face. There was a slight pause before it began again. The dark browed one danced up and down and whipped the rope around my shoulders and body with the force of the blow. Then it would be a moment before he could pull it away. The raw pain surged through my whole body, reached down and pierced my legs and my finger tips with each slash of the doubled rope, now wet with blood. I gasped and gagged for the breath which seemed burned out of me. I kept my lips tight shut, but I couldn't stop the grunts that came with each blow . . .

I don't know when it stopped. I only know that I could think of nothing but the great necessity of keeping my mouth shut and lying as still as possible. I recall more questions coming out of the shadows, through the whisper of the descending rope, the eternal convulsions of pain. There was nothing more important in the world, nothing else in the world at that time, but this.

Vaguely I realized that it had stopped, heard the car door slam, and tried to lift my head as the tires dug into the soft dirt and the car spun away. I tried to see the license number in the moonlight, but a mist hung over my right eye. The left was useless, buried under great puffs of swollen flesh.

I let my face drop forward·again, and hugged the earth, not wanting to slip off into sleep, wanting now to go, somehow, back to Birmingham, back to the workers there.

Workers kept an armed vigil at my bedside. One metal worker, who had been a member of the Klan only a few years ago, brought his little eight-year-old boy to me. He asked me to sit up in bed, and he bared the cuts and slashes that crisscrossed my body, back and face, before the child's eyes.

"Look at that, sonny," he said. "That's the company. That's what you got to learn to hate — and fight agin."

BLAINE OWEN, in *The New Republic*, *Aug. 28, 1935.*
(Reprinted by permission.)

REFERENCE NOTES

To date the record of the hearings of the La Follette Committee has been published in eight volumes: one covering the preliminary hearings and eight others covering the hearings thereafter. The volume of the preliminary hearings is referred to throughout as Prelim and the succeeding volumes are referred to by their Roman numerals.

REFERENCE NOTES

Chapter I

Pages 3, 4. IV, p. 1262 ff.

Page 5, line 10. Ibid., p. 1388.

Page 6, line 6. Prelim., p. 72.
Line 14. Ibid., p. 77 (in the larger figure there was no attempt to draw the line between spies and strike-breakers).
Line 23. Ibid., p. 77.
Line 28. VI, pp. 2175, 2186.

Page 7, line 25. Prelim., p. 336 (this list includes hirers of the strike-breaking service of detective agencies).

Page 8, line 7. IV, pp. 1363–1370.
Line 16. V, pp. 1853–1857.
Line 27. I, pp. 292–294.

Chapter II

Page 10, line 15. Prelim., p. 60.

Page 11, line 17. Jean E. Spielman, *The Stool-Pigeon and the Open Shop Movement*, p. 39. American Publishing Co., Minneapolis, 1923.
Line 27. IV, p. 1105.

Page 12, line 5. Prelim., p. 68.
Line 24. IV, p. 1105.

Page 13, line 15. Ibid., pp. 1211, 1213.

Page 17, line 13. V, pp. 1612–1614.

Page 18, line 28. Ibid., pp. 1515, 1516.

Page 19, line 29. Ibid., p. 1538.

Page 20, line 32. VI, pp. 2103, 2104.

Page 21, line 8. VII, p. 2318.
Line 21. Prelim., p. 104.

Page 22, line 29. Ibid., p. 311.

Page 23, line 5. Ibid., pp. 275, 310.
Line 17. *New York Times*, December 17, 1934.
Line 22. IV, p. 1148.

Page 24, line 21. V, p. 1616 (my arrangement).

Page 25, line 8. IV, p. 1376.

Page 26, line 3. V, pp. 1608, 1609.
Line 20. National Labor Relations Act (48 Stat. 449), 74th Congress. Approved July 5, 1935.

Page 27, line 12. Prelim., p. 275.

Page 28, line 4. II, p. 686 ff.
Line 22. Prelim., p. 291.

Page 29, line 2. Ibid., p. 292.
Line 31. Ibid., p. 22.

Page 30, line 14. Ibid., p. 318.
Line 24. Quoted in *The New Republic*, March 3, 1937.

Page 31, line 2. Prelim., p. 69.
Line 19. I, pp. 71, 72.

Page 32, line 22. Ibid., pp. 179, 180.

Page 33, line 10. Ibid., p. 205.
Line 34. VI, p. 2069.

Chapter III

Page 36, line 14. Prelim., p. 163.

Page 39, line 12. III, p. 1060.

Page 41, line 7. Ibid., p. 1061.

Page 43, line 3. IV, p. 1432.

Page 44, line 2. Ibid., pp. 1432, 1433.

Page 45, line 3. Ibid., pp. 1442, 1443.
Line 13. Ibid., p. 1312.
Line 16. Ibid., p. 1312.

Page 46, line 7. Ibid., p. 1317.
Line 14. Ibid., p. 1315.
Line 34. Ibid., pp. 1434, 1435.

Page 49, line 18. Ibid., pp. 1436, 1437.

Chapter IV

Page 52, line 20. I, p. 201.
Line 36. IV, p. 1420.

Page 53, line 22. Ibid., p. 1273.
Line 26. I, p. 182.
Page 54, line 8. Ibid., p. 42.
Line 14. Ibid., p. 81.
Page 55, line 4. Ibid., p. 43.
Page 57, line 28. IV, pp. 1317–1319.
Page 59, line 34. Ibid., pp. 1320–1322.
Page 60, line 12. II, p. 503.
Page 61, line 9. IV, p. 1423.
Page 63, line 2. Prelim., p. 17.
Line 23. Ibid., p. 177.
Page 64, line 2. V, p. 1477.
Line 34. IV, p. 1149.
Page 65, line 18. Ibid., pp. 1377, 1378.
Page 68, line 14. Ibid., pp. 1384, 1385.
Page 69, line 26. Ibid., pp. 1435, 1436.

CHAPTER V

Page 71, line 19. IV, p. 1348.
Page 72, line 14. Ibid., p. 111 1 ff.
Line 19. II, pp. 674, 675.
Line 24. Ibid., p. 494.
Page 73, line 7. Ibid., p. 474 ff.
Page 75, line 34. Prelim., pp. 334, 335.
Page 76, line 20. IV, p. 1349 ff.
Line 28. Ibid., p. 1349 ff.
Page 77, line 17. Ibid., pp. 1118, 1119.
Page 78, line 24. Ibid., p. 1161.
Page 79, line 17. V, p. 1866.
Page 81, line 18. VI, pp. 1916–1918.
Page 82, line 20. IV, pp. 1222, 1227.
Page 83, line 3. VI, p. 1916.
Line 24. Ibid., pp. 1978–1981.
Page 84, line 25. VIII, p. 2843.
Page 85, line 30. Ibid., p. 2775.
Page 87, line 32. V, pp. 1513, 1514.
Page 90, line 28. Ibid., pp. 1519–1528.
Page 91, line 8. Ibid., p. 1589.
Page 92, line 9. Ibid., pp. 1590, 1591.
Line 32. IV, p. 1176.
Page 93, line 5. Ibid., p. 1177.
Line 12. VI, p. 2061.
Line 14. IV, ⌐p. 1153–1160.
Line 16. V, p. 1540.

Page 94, line 7. II, 594.
Line 26. Ibid., pp. 399, 400.
Page 95, line 15. I, p. 268.
Page 96, line 21. Prelim., pp. 177, 178.
Page 97, line 15. Congressional Record,
April 7, 1937, p. 4132.
Line 32. V, pp. 1534, 1535.
Page 98, line 14. I, p. 202.
Line 30. Jean E. Spielman, op. cit., p. 239.
Page 99, line 12. II, p. 390.
Line 19. Ibid., p. 391.
Line 29. Ibid., p. 392.
Page 100, line 7. Ibid., p. 655.
Page 101, line 9. Ibid., pp. 402, 403.
Line 34. Ibid., p. 595.
Page 102, line 7. Ibid., p. 383.
Line 32. I, p. 79.

CHAPTER VI

Page 105, line 9. Adam Smith, *An Inquiry into the Nature and Causes of the Wealth of Nations*, pp. 70, 71, edited by C. J. Bullock. Harvard Classics edition, Collier & Son, 1909.
Line 21. C. E. Bonnett, *Employers Associations in the United States*, p. 14. The Macmillan Company, N. Y., 1922.
Page 107, line 3. VIII, pp. 3086–3090.
Page 110, line 4. Ibid., pp. 2954–2958.
Line 32. Ibid., pp. 2947, 2948.
Page 112, lihe 11. Ibid., pp. 2948–2950.
Page 113, line 29. Ibid., pp. 2958–2962.
Page 114, line 11. Ibid., p. 2952.
Line 24. Ibid., p. 2952.
Page 115, line 28. Ibid., pp. 3198, 3199.
Page 118, line 2. VIII, pp. 2881, 2882.
Page 119, line 3. III, pp. 981–994.
Line 17. Ibid., pp. 818, 820.
Page 120, line 13. Ibid., p. 1007.
Line 22. Ibid., p. 1007.
Page 121, line 3. Ibid., p. 1007.
Page 122, line 8. Ibid., pp. 833, 834.
Page 123, line 3. Ibid., pp. 835, 836.

Page 125, line 2. Ibid., pp. 901, 902.
Line 31. Ibid., p. 889.
Page 126, line 31. Ibid., p. 890.
Page 127, line 17. Ibid., p. 945.
Page 128, line 3. Ibid., p. 936.
Line 20. Ibid., p. 887.
Page 129, line 12. II, p. 404.
Page 130, line 23. III, pp. 939–941.
Page 131, line 17. Ibid., p. 911.
Line 22. Ibid., p. 912.
Page 132, line 12. Ibid., p. 913.
Page 133, line 15. Ibid., pp. 915, 916.
Line 34. Ibid., p. 917.
Page 134, line 11. C. E. Bonnett, op. cit., p. 292.
Line 16. Ibid., p. 295.
Page 136, line 4. Cf. Harry A. Bullis, *Industry Must Speak*. Published by National Association of Manufactures, N. Y., 1936, pp. 9–13.
Line 9. Ibid., p. 13.
Page 137, line 22. VI, p. 2036.

CHAPTER VII

Page 140, line 9. IV, p. 1273.
Line 31. National Labor Relations Board v. Jones & Laughlin Steel Corporation, *The New York Times*, April 13, 1937.
Page 141, line 5. Holden v. Hardy, 169 U. S. pp. 366, 397.
Page 142, line 3. Quoted in National Labor Relations Board, Division of Economic Research, Bulletin No. 1, pp. 82, 83, Government Printing Office, August, 1936.
Line 16. Cf. *Monthly Labor Review*, Bureau of Labor Statistics, U. S. Dept. of Labor, Jan., 1936, May, 1936, May, 1937.
Page 143, line 2. National Labor Relations Board v. Jones & Laughlin Steel Corporation, op. cit.
Line 15. *The New York Herald Tribune*, February 10, 1937.
Line 33. Ibid., March 6, 1937.

Page 144, line 7. VII, p. 2509.
Line 21. *The New York Times*, March 15, 1937.
Page 145, line 10. III, p. 883.
Line 22. Prelim., p. 47.
Page 146, line 15. *The New York Times*, April 14, 1937.
Page 147, line 7. Ibid., December 17, 1934.
Line 30. Ibid., May 27, 1937.
Page 148, line 4. Ibid., May 27, 1937.
Line 35. Ibid., June 1, 1937.
Page 149, line 7. *The New York Post*, June 17, 1937.
Page 150, line 24. Prelim., pp. 267, 268.
Page 151, line 3. III, p. 752.
Line 13. Ibid., p. 1048.
Line 16. IV, p. 1341.
Page 152, line 7. VIII, pp. 2983, 2984.
Page 153, line 17. Ibid., pp. 2995, 2996.
Page 154, line 11. Ibid., p. 2975.
Line 28. II, p. 410.
Page 155, line 6. Ibid., pp. 410, 411.
Line 20. Ibid., p. 393.
Line 24. Ibid., p. 390.
Line 26. Ibid., p. 458.

CHAPTER VIII

Page 159, line 4. III, p. 862.
Line 20. C. E. Bonnett, op. cit., p. 80.
Line 25. IV, p. 1282.
Line 30. Prelim., p. 7.
Page 160, line 6. National Labor Relations Board v. Jones & Laughlin Steel Corporation, op. cit.
Line 30. National Labor Relations Act, op. cit.
Page 161, line 26. National Labor Relations Board, Bulletin No. 1, op. cit., p. 83.
Page 162, line 14. Congressional Record, April 7, 1937, p. 4119.
Page 163, line 7. *The New York Times*, Feb. 14, 1937.
Line 11. Henry D. Lloyd, *Wealth against Commonwealth* (1894), p. 175. National Home Library Foundation, Washington, D. C., 1936.

INDEX

A.

Adlen, Richard, spy, affidavits on, 46.
Ailes, A. S., 94, 128, 129, 154, 155.
  testimony of, 100, 101.
Agencies, clients of, 7.
  evasion of Social Security Act by, 92, 93.
  formation of company unions by, 30–33.
  list of, Appendix A.
  making and faking of trouble by, 95 ff.
  morals and ethics of, 71 ff.
  new technique for strike-breaking, 115–118.
  number of, 5.
  relation to class war of, 143.
  spying on spies by, 84.
  spying on vendor plants by, 81–83.
  strike-breaking by, 99, 100.
  tie-up to munitions firms of, 102, 104.
  tools of employers, 139 ff.
  trustification of, 103, 104.
Akron *Beacon-Journal*, editorial of, 114, 115.
Akron Law and Order League, 114, 115.
American Federation of Labor, questionnaire of, 21, 22.
American Liberty League, 26.
"American Way," the, 139 ff.
Anderson, Harry W., testimony of, 81.
Andrews, John, 71.
—— and Richard Frankensteen, 3–4.
Associations of employers, number of, 105 ff.
  purpose of, 105 ff.
Atlantic Production Co., 66, 67.

B.

Babson, Roger W., report on agencies of, 98.

B.

Barker, Lawrence, testimony of, 20.
Bennett, Harry H., 146, 147.
Blacklist, 28.
Black and Decker Electric Co., strike at, 129, 130.
Blankenhorn, Heber, 5, 6.
Blind Ads, 64, 65.
Bonnett, Clarence E., 105.
Brady, Samuel H., 63.
Bronson, R. L., 55–57.
Brunswick, R. L., 86.
Bullis, Harry A., 134, 136.
Burns, William J., International Detective Agency, Inc., 6.
  shadowing of trial jurors by, 84, 85.
Burns, W. Sherman, letter of solicitation, 106, 107.
  testimony of, 84, 85.
Burnside, R. L., testimony of, 58, 59, 88–90.
Butler, System of Industrial Survey, 30, 31.

C.

Caldwell, Frank W., 132.
Capital and Labor, strength of, 141.
Chrysler Corp., 12.
  payment to Corporations Auxiliary Co., 5, 76.
  Securities Act violation by, 76–78.
Citizens' Alliance groups, purpose of 115–118.
Clark, Edward S., testimony of, 83.
Class war, 139 ff.
  indication of, 143 ff.
Coates, Robert W., testimony of, 83, 84.
Collective bargaining, 160, 161.
  statement of Commission on Industrial Relations on, 161.